Praise for *Functional Programming in Java*

Venkat has done a superb job of bringing core functional language concepts to the Java ecosystem. Once you have peered into his looking glass of functional language design, it will be hard to go back to old-school imperative programming.

➤ **Stephen Chin, Java technology ambassador and JavaOne content chair**

The introduction of lambdas to Java 8 has made me excited to use Java again, and Venkat's combination of technical details and best practices make it easy to apply functional thinking to this new feature.

➤ **Kimberly D. Barnes, senior software engineer**

Java 8 lambda expressions are an incredibly important new language feature. Every Java developer should read this excellent book and learn how to use them effectively.

➤ **Chris Richardson, software architect and Java champion**

Many can explain lambdas; Venkat makes them useful.

➤ **Kirk Pepperdine, Java performance tuning expert**

I highly recommend this book for Java programmers who want to get up to speed with functional programming in Java 8. It is a very concise book but still provides a comprehensive overview of Java 8.

➤ **Nilanjan Raychaudhuri, author and developer at Typesafe**

Functional Programming in Java

Harnessing the Power of Java 8 Lambda Expressions

Venkat Subramaniam

The Pragmatic Bookshelf

Dallas, Texas • Raleigh, North Carolina

Our Pragmatic courses, workshops, and other products can help you and your team create better software and have more fun. For more information, as well as the latest Pragmatic titles, please visit us at *http://pragprog.com*.

Sir Charles Antony Richard Hoare's quote is used by permission of the ACM.
Abelson and Sussman's quote is used under Creative Commons license.

The team that produced this book includes:

Jacquelyn Carter (editor)
Potomac Indexing, LLC (indexer)
Candace Cunningham (copyeditor)
David J Kelly (typesetter)
Janet Furlow (producer)
Ellie Callahan (support)

For international rights, please contact *rights@pragprog.com*.

Printed in the United States of America.
ISBN-13: 978-1-937785-46-8
Printed on acid-free paper.
Book version: P1.0—February 2014

To the loving memory of my grandmothers,
Kuppammal and Jayalakshmi. I cherish my
wonder years under your care.

Contents

Foreword

Venkat Subramaniam would never be described as a "waterfall" sort of guy. So, when he mentioned that he was starting on a Java 8 book—long before the design of Java 8 was settled—I was not at all surprised. It was clear this was going to be an "agile" book project.

Despite having to more than occasionally rework the text as the language and library features evolved, Venkat had a secret advantage—he knew where we were going. The Java 8 design was heavily influenced by the core principles of functional programming: functions as values, immutability, and statelessness. We didn't do this because functional programming is trendy or cool; we did it because programs that are expressed as stateless transformations on immutable data, rather than as modifications of mutable data structures, tend to be easier to read and maintain, to be less error prone, and to parallelize more gracefully.

The new features introduced in Java 8 were designed together to facilitate development of more expressive and parallel-friendly libraries. Lambda expressions reduce the syntactic overhead of encoding behavior as data; default methods allow existing libraries to evolve over time, enabling core JDK classes such as Collections to take advantage of lambda expressions; the java.util.stream package leverages these language features to offer rich aggregate operations on collections, arrays, and other data sources in a declarative, expressive, and parallel-friendly manner. All of this adds up to more powerful and performant code, as well as a more pleasant programming experience.

This book not only provides lots of examples of how to use these new features, but offers readers a peek into the underlying principles behind their design, and *why* they result in better code. Let Venkat be your guide to this new and improved Java—you're in for a treat.

Brian Goetz
Java Language Architect, Oracle Corporation
September 2013

Acknowledgments

Writing a book is like taking a road trip—we know where we're heading, but some details emerge only after the start. The journey may involve detours—opportunities to explore unexpected places—and it's more fun with good company. I'm thankful for the great company of people on this voyage: smart reviewers, an amazing editor, a wonderful set of people at The Pragmatic Bookshelf, and a very supportive family.

I first thank the Java language team members at Oracle for their hard work to bring the functional style of programming to one of the most popular mainstream languages. You've taken the language in the right direction—not through shortcuts and quick fixes, but by way of sound reasoning and prudent design decisions. Kudos, team.

I express my sincere gratitude to the smart developers who volunteered their personal time to review this book. Thank you, Kimberly Barnes, Fred Daoud, Raju Gandhi, Marty Hall, Praveen Kumar, Rebecca Parsons, Kirk Pepperdine, Chris Richardson, Ian Roughley, Nate Schutta, Ken Sipe, and Dan Sline. Your comments were critical yet very constructive and motivational; they helped make this book better. I'm honored and humbled by Bruce Tate reviewing this book. He's been a great mentor for me over the years. He reviewed this book multiple times, at different stages, and took the time to motivate me as to why certain changes were essential. Thank you, Bruce. I'd also like to express my gratitude to Brian Goetz for reviewing the book multiple times, for the encouragement starting early on, and for kindly agreeing to write the foreword. Any errors in the book are solely mine.

The biggest benefit of publishing a beta copy of a book is the opportunity to improve it based on valuable feedback from early readers. I'm indebted to the following readers for taking their valuable time to provide feedback on the forum for this book or reporting errors on the errata page. Thank you, Greg Helton, Günter Jantzen, Narayanan Jayaratchagan, Wacek Kusnierczyk, Nabeel Ali Memon, Marc-Daniel Ortega, Arjo Ouwens, Philip Schwarz,

Ekaterina Sh, Dan Talpau, Benjamin Tan, Brian Tarbox, Marco Vermeulen, and Jason Weden.

I benefited greatly from every interaction with Jackie Carter. She did not just edit; she motivated me and helped shape this book. Thank you, Jackie, for your hard work, fast responses, and truly making this a fun experience.

Impatience is one of my many weaknesses, but the kind folks at The Pragmatic Bookshelf turned that into a strength when I set out to write this book. Susannah Pfalzer, Andy Hunt, Dave Thomas, and several others worked behind the scenes to help me succeed on a self-imposed fast-paced schedule. You make writing books so much easier and more fun, much more than you may realize.

I have enjoyed the privilege of being part of various conferences, and the No Fluff Just Stuff (NFJS) conference series in particular. I have learned a lot from the interactions I've had with other speakers and developers. Special thanks to my friends on the conference circuit, especially Jay Zimmerman, director of NFJS.

I thank my wife Kavitha and sons Karthik and Krupa for letting me hide in my office during the holidays to work on this book. It was a true pleasure to have their support and above all to see their curiousness. Special thanks to my parents for their blessings and encouragement.

In any field, find the strangest thing and then explore it.

> ➤ *John Archibald Wheeler*

Preface

You're in for a treat. One of the most prominent and widely used languages in the world has evolved. Until now Java gave us one set of tools—the object-oriented paradigm—and we did the best we could with it. Now there's another, more elegant way to solve the common problems we encounter when developing applications. We can now do quite effectively in Java what was previously possible only on the JVM using other languages—this means more power to Java programmers.

I'm thankful to have had the privilege over the past few decades to program with multiple languages: C, C++, Java, C#, F#, Ruby, Groovy, Scala, Clojure, Erlang, JavaScript... When asked which one's my favorite, my resounding answer has been that it's not the language that excites me, but the way we program.

The science and engineering in programming drew me in, but the art in programming keeps me. Coding has a lot in common with writing—there's more than one way to express our ideas. Java helped us write code using objects. Now we have an additional way to implement our designs and ideas.

This is a new way in Java, one that will make our code more expressive, easier to write, less error prone, and easier to parallelize than has been the case with Java until now. This way has been around for decades and widely used in languages like Lisp, Clojure, Erlang, Smalltalk, Scala, Groovy, and Ruby. It's not only a new way in Java, but a better way.

Since coding is like writing, we can learn a few things from that field. In *On Writing Well [Zin01]*, William Zinsser recommends simplicity, clarity, and brevity. To create better applications, we can start by making the code simpler, clear, and concise. The new style of programming in Java lets us do exactly that, as we will explore throughout this book.

Who's This Book For

This book is for programmers well versed in object-oriented programming in Java and keen to learn and apply the new facilities of lambda expressions. You'll need good experience programming in previous versions of Java, especially Java 5, to make the best use of this book.

Programmers mostly interested in JVM languages like Scala, Groovy, JRuby, and Clojure can benefit from the examples in this book and can relate back to the facilities offered in those languages. They can also use the examples to help fellow Java programmers on their teams.

Programmers experienced with the functional style of programming in other languages and who are now involved in Java projects can use this book, as well. They can learn how what they know translates to the specifics of the lambda expressions' usage in Java.

Programmers who are familiar with lambda expressions in Java can use this book to help coach and train their team members who are getting up to speed in this area.

What's in This Book

This book will help you get up to speed with Java 8 lambda expressions, to think in the elegant style, and to benefit from the additions to the Java Development Kit (JDK) library. We'll take an example-driven approach to exploring the concepts. Rather than discuss the theory of functional programming, we'll dive into specific day-to-day tasks to apply the elegant style. This approach will quickly get these concepts under our belts so we can put them to real use on projects right away.

On the first read, take the time to go over the chapters sequentially as we build upon previously discussed concepts and examples. Each chapter closes with a quick summary to recap what was covered. Later, when working on applications, take a quick glance at any relevant example or section in the book. There's also a syntax appendix for quick reference.

Here's how the rest of the book is organized:

We discuss the functional style of programming, its benefits, and how it differs from the prevalent imperative style in Chapter 1, *Hello, Lambda Expressions!*, on page 1. We also look into how Java supports lambda expressions in this chapter.

The JDK collections have received some special treatment in Java 8, with new interfaces, classes, and methods that support functional-style operations. We will explore these in Chapter 2, *Using Collections*, on page 19.

In Chapter 3, *Strings, Comparators, and Filters*, on page 41, we exploit functional-style and lambda expressions to work with strings, implement the Comparator interface, and use filters for file selection.

In addition to using the functional-style facilities in the JDK, we can benefit from applying the elegant style in the design of methods and classes we create. We'll cover functional-style design techniques in Chapter 4, *Designing with Lambda Expressions*, on page 63.

The lambda expressions facilitate a code structure that helps delineate operations to manage object lifetimes and resource cleanup, as we'll discuss in Chapter 5, *Working with Resources*, on page 87.

We'll see lambda expressions shine in Chapter 6, *Being Lazy*, on page 103; they provide us the ability to postpone instance creation and method evaluations as well as create infinite lazy collections, and thereby improve the code's performance.

In Chapter 7, *Optimizing Recursions*, on page 121, we will use lambda expressions to optimize recursions and achieve stellar performance using memoization techniques.

We'll put the techniques we cover in the book to some real use in Chapter 8, *Composing with Lambda Expressions*, on page 135, where we'll transform objects, implement MapReduce, and safely parallelize a program with little effort.

In Chapter 9, *Bringing It All Together*, on page 147, we'll go over the key concepts and the practices needed to adopt those techniques.

In Appendix 1, *Starter Set of Functional Interfaces*, on page 155, we'll take a glance at some of the most popular functional interfaces.

A quick overview of the Java 8 syntax for functional interfaces, lambda expressions, and method/constructor references is in Appendix 2, *Syntax Overview*, on page 157.

The URLs mentioned throughout this book are gathered together for your convenience in Appendix 3, *Web Resources*, on page 163.

Java Version Used in This Book

To run the examples in this book you need Java 8 with support for lambda expressions. Using automated scripts, the examples in this book have been tried out with the following version of Java:

```
java version "1.8.0"
Java(TM) SE Runtime Environment (build 1.8.0-b128)
Java HotSpot(TM) 64-Bit Server VM (build 25.0-b69, mixed mode)
```

Take a few minutes to download the appropriate version of Java for your system. This will help you follow along with the examples in this book.

How to Read the Code Examples

When writing code in Java, we place classes in packages, and executable statements and expressions in methods. To reduce clutter, we'll skip the package names and imports in the code listings. All code in this book belongs to a package:

```
package fpij;
```

Any executable code not listed within a method is part of an undisplayed main() method. When going through the code listings, if you have an urge to look at the full source code, remember it's only a click away at the website for this book.

Online Resources

A number of web resources referenced throughout the book are collected in Appendix 3, *Web Resources*, on page 163. Here are a few that will help you get started with this book:

The Oracle website for downloading the version of Java used in this book is https://jdk8.java.net/download.html. The JDK documentation is available at http://download.java.net/jdk8/docs/api.

This book's page at the Pragmatic Bookshelf website is http://www.pragprog.com/titles/vsjava8. From there you can download all the example source code for the book. You can also provide feedback by submitting errata entries or posting your comments and questions in the forum. If you're reading the book in PDF form, you can click on the link above a code listing to view or download the specific examples.

Now for some fun with lambda expressions...

Venkat Subramaniam

February 2014

CHAPTER 1

Hello, Lambda Expressions!

Our Java coding style is ready for a remarkable makeover.

The everyday tasks we perform just got simpler, easier, and more expressive.
The new way of programming in Java has been around for decades in other
languages. With these facilities in Java we can write concise, elegant, and
expressive code with fewer errors. We can use this to easily enforce policies
and implement common design patterns with fewer lines of code.

In this book we'll explore the functional style of programming using direct
examples of everyday tasks we do as programmers. Before we take the leap
to this elegant style, and this new way to design and program, let's discuss
why it's better.

Change the Way You Think

Imperative style—that's what Java has provided us since its inception. In this
style, we tell Java every step of what we want it to do and then we watch it
faithfully exercise those steps. That's worked fine, but it's a bit low level. The
code tends to get verbose, and we often wish the language were a tad more
intelligent; we could then tell it—declaratively—*what* we want rather than
delve into *how* to do it. Thankfully, Java can now help us do that. Let's look
at a few examples to see the benefits and the differences in style.

The Habitual Way

Let's start on familiar ground to see the two paradigms in action. Here's an
imperative way to find if Chicago is in a collection of given cities—remember, the

---

1. Hoare, Charles Antony Richard, "The Emperor's Old Clothes," *Communications of the
   ACM* 24, no. 2 (February 1981): 5–83, doi:10.1145/358549.358561.

listings in this book only have snippets of code (see *How to Read the Code Examples*, on page xviii).

```
introduction/fpij/Cities.java
boolean found = false;
for(String city : cities) {
  if(city.equals("Chicago")) {
    found = true;
    break;
  }
}

System.out.println("Found chicago?:" + found);
```

This imperative version is noisy and low level; it has several moving parts. We first initialize a smelly boolean flag named found and then walk through each element in the collection. If we found the city we're looking for, then we set the flag and break out of the loop. Finally we print out the result of our finding.

A Better Way

As observant Java programmers, the minute we set our eyes on this code we'd quickly turn it into something more concise and easier to read, like this:

```
introduction/fpij/Cities.java
System.out.println("Found chicago?:" + cities.contains("Chicago"));
```

That's one example of declarative style—the contains() method helped us get directly to our business.

Tangible Improvements

That change improved our code in quite a few ways:

- No messing around with mutable variables
- Iteration steps wrapped under the hood
- Less clutter
- Better clarity; retains our focus
- Less impedance; code closely trails the business intent
- Less error prone
- Easier to understand and maintain

Beyond Simple Cases

That was simple—the declarative function to check if an element is present in a collection has been around in Java for a very long time. Now imagine not having to write imperative code for more advanced operations, like parsing files, working with databases, making calls to web services, *programming concurrency*, and so on. Java now makes it possible to write concise, elegant, less error-prone code, not just for simple cases, but throughout our applications.

The Old Way

Let's look at another example. We'll define a collection of prices and try out a few ways to total discounted price values.

```
final List<BigDecimal> prices = Arrays.asList(
  new BigDecimal("10"), new BigDecimal("30"), new BigDecimal("17"),
  new BigDecimal("20"), new BigDecimal("15"), new BigDecimal("18"),
  new BigDecimal("45"), new BigDecimal("12"));
```

Suppose we're asked to total the prices greater than $20, discounted by 10%. Let's do that in the habitual Java way first.

```
introduction/fpij/DiscountImperative.java
BigDecimal totalOfDiscountedPrices = BigDecimal.ZERO;

for(BigDecimal price : prices) {
  if(price.compareTo(BigDecimal.valueOf(20)) > 0)
    totalOfDiscountedPrices =
      totalOfDiscountedPrices.add(price.multiply(BigDecimal.valueOf(0.9)));
}
System.out.println("Total of discounted prices: " + totalOfDiscountedPrices);
```

That's familiar code; we start with a mutable variable to hold the total of the discounted prices. We then loop through the prices, pick each price greater than $20, compute each item's discounted value, and add those to the total. Finally we print the total value of the discounted prices.

And here's the output from the code.

```
Total of discounted prices: 67.5
```

It worked, but writing it feels dirty. It's no fault of ours; we had to use what was available. But the code is fairly low level—it suffers from "primitive obsession" and defies the single-responsibility principle. Those of us working from home have to keep this code away from the eyes of kids aspiring to be programmers, for they may be dismayed and sigh, "That's what you do for a living?"

A Better Way, Again

Now we can do better—a lot better. Our code can resemble the requirement specification. This will help reduce the gap between the business needs and the code that implements it, further reducing the chances of the requirements being misinterpreted.

Rather than tell Java to create a mutable variable and then to repeatedly assign to it, let's talk with it at a higher level of abstraction, as in the next code.

```
introduction/fpij/DiscountFunctional.java
final BigDecimal totalOfDiscountedPrices =
  prices.stream()
        .filter(price -> price.compareTo(BigDecimal.valueOf(20)) > 0)
        .map(price -> price.multiply(BigDecimal.valueOf(0.9)))
        .reduce(BigDecimal.ZERO, BigDecimal::add);

System.out.println("Total of discounted prices: " + totalOfDiscountedPrices);
```

Let's read that aloud—filter prices greater than $20, map the prices to discounted values, and then add them up. The code flows along with logic in the same way we'd describe the requirements. As a convention in Java, we wrap long lines of code and line up the dots before the method names, as in the previous example.

The code is concise, but we're using quite a number of new things from Java 8. First, we invoked a stream() method on the prices list. This opens the door to a *special* iterator with a wealth of convenience functions, which we'll discuss later.

Instead of explicitly iterating through the prices list, we're using a few special methods, such as filter() and map(). Unlike the methods we're used to in Java and the Java Development Kit (JDK), these methods take an anonymous function—a lambda expression—as a parameter, within the parentheses (). (We'll soon explore this further.) We invoke the reduce() method to compute the total on the result of the map() method.

The looping is concealed much like it was under the contains() method. The map() method (and the filter() method), however, is more sophisticated. For each price in the prices list, it invokes the provided lambda expression and puts the responses from these calls into a new collection. The reduce() method is invoked on this collection to get the final result.

Here's the output from this version of code:

```
Total of discounted prices: 67.5
```

The Improvements

This is quite an improvement from the habitual way:

- Nicely composed, not cluttered
- Free of low-level operations
- Easier to enhance or change the logic
- Iteration controlled by a library of methods
- Efficient; lazy evaluation of loops
- Easier to parallelize where desired

Later we'll discuss how Java provides these improvements.

Lambdas to the Rescue

Lambdas are the functional key to free us from the hassles of imperative programming. By changing the way we program, with a feature now baked into Java, we can write code that's not only elegant and concise, but also less prone to errors; more efficient; and easier to optimize, enhance, and parallelize.

The Big Gains of Functional-Style Code

Functional-style code has a higher signal-to-noise ratio; we write fewer lines of code, but each line or expression achieves more. We gained quite a bit from the functional-style version, compared with the imperative-style version:

- We avoided explicit mutation or reassignment of variables, which are often sources of bugs and result in code that's hard to make concurrent. In the imperative version we repeatedly set the totalOfDiscountedPrices variable within the loop. In the functional-style version, there is no explicit mutation in our code. Fewer mutations leads to fewer errors in code.

- The functional version can easily be parallelized. If the computation was time consuming, we can easily run it concurrently for each element in the list. If we parallelized the imperative version, we'd have to worry about concurrent modification of the totalOfDiscountedPrices variable. In the functional version we gain access to the variable only after it's fully baked, which removes the thread-safety concerns.

- The code is more expressive. Rather than conveying the intent in multiple steps—create an initial dummy value, loop through prices, add discounted values to the variable, and so on—we simply ask the list's map() method to return another list with discounted values, and sum it.

- The functional-style version is more concise; it took us fewer lines of code to achieve the same result as the imperative version. More concise code means less code to write, less code to read, and less code to maintain— see *Does concise just mean less code?*, on page 7.

- The functional-style version is intuitive—code reads more like how we'd state the problem—and it's easier to understand once we're familiar with the syntax. The map() method applies the given function (which computes the discount) to each element of the collection and produces the resulting collection, as we see in the following figure.

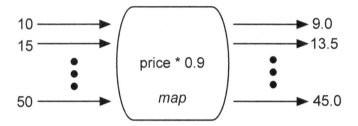

Figure 1—map applies the given function on each element of the collection.

With the support for lambda expressions, we can fully utilize the power of the functional style of programming in Java. If we embrace this style, we can create more expressive, more concise code with less mutability and fewer errors.

One of Java's key strengths has been its support of the object-oriented paradigm. The functional style is not counter to object-oriented programming (OOP). The real paradigm shift is from the imperative to the declarative style of programming. With Java 8, we can now intermix functional and OO styles of programming quite effectively. We can continue to use the OOP style to model domain entities, their states, and their relationships. In addition, we can model the behavior or state transformations, business workflows, and data processing as a series of functions to form a function composition.

Why Code in the Functional Style?

We saw the general benefits of the functional style of programming, but is it worth picking up this new style? Should we expect a marginal improvement, or is it life altering? Those are genuine questions that we need answered before we commit our time and effort.

Writing Java code is not that hard; the syntax is simple. We've gotten quite familiar and comfortable with the libraries and their APIs. What really gets us is the effort required to code and maintain the typical enterprise applications we use Java to develop.

\//
ッ
    Joe asks:
Does concise just mean less code?

Concise is short, devoid of noise, and boiled down to its essence to convey the intent effectively. The benefits are far reaching.

Writing code is like throwing ingredients together; making it concise is like turning that into a sauce. It often takes more effort to write concise code. It's less code to read, but effective code is transparent. A short code listing that's hard to understand or hides details is *terse* rather than *concise*.

Concise code equals design agility. Concise code has less ceremony.[a] This means we can quickly try out our design ideas and move forward if they're good, or move on if they turn sour.

---

a.   Stuart Halloway on essence versus ceremony: http://thinkrelevance.com/blog/2008/04/01/ending-legacy-code-in-our-lifetime.

We must ensure that fellow programmers have closed the database connections at the right time, that they're not holding on to transactions any longer than needed, that they're handling the exceptions well and at the right level, that they're securing and releasing locks properly...and the list goes on.

Each one of these in isolation may not seem like a big deal. But when combined with the domain's inherent complexities, things get quite overwhelming, labor intensive, and hard to maintain.

What if we could encapsulate each of these decisions into tiny pieces of code that can manage the constraints well? Then we wouldn't have to continuously expend energy to enforce policies. That would be a big win, so let's see how the functional style can help.

Iteration on Steroids

We write iterations all the time to process a list of objects and to work with sets and maps. The iterators we're used to in Java are familiar and primitive, but not simple. Not only do they take a few lines of code to work with; they're also quite hard to compose.

How do we iterate and print each element in a collection? We could use a for loop. How do we select some elements from a collection? With the same for loop, but some extra mutable variables have to step in to support the operation. Now after selecting the values, how do we reduce the results to a single value, such as a minimum, a maximum, or an average? More looping, more mutable variables.

That's like having a jack-of-all-iterations, but a master of none. Java now provides specialized internal iterators for various operations: one to simply loop, one to map data values, one to filter out select values, one to reduce, and several convenience functions to pick the min, the max, the average, and so on. In addition, these operations nicely compose so we can combine a variety of them to implement the business logic with greater ease and less code. When we're done, the code is easier to understand, as it logically flows thought the sequence described in the problem. We'll see several examples of this in Chapter 2, *Using Collections*, on page 19, and throughout the book.

Enforcing Policies

Policies rule enterprise applications. For instance, we may have to ensure an operation has proper security credentials. We may have to ensure that transactions run fast and update audit trails properly. These tasks often turn into mundane service-tier code like the following pseudocode form:

```
Transaction transaction = getFromTransactionFactory();

//... operation to run within the transaction ...

checkProgressAndCommitOrRollbackTransaction();
UpdateAuditTrail();
```

There are two issues with this kind of approach. First, it often leads to duplication of effort and, in turn, increases maintenance cost. Second, it's easy to forget about exceptions that may be thrown in the application code, thus jeopardizing the transaction lifetime and the update of audit trails. We could implement a proper try and finally block, but every time someone touches that code, we'd have to reverify that it's not broken.

Alternatively, we could get rid of the factory and turn this code on its head. Instead of receiving a transaction, we could send the processing code to a well-managed function, like so (in pseudocode):

```
runWithinTransaction((Transaction transaction) -> {
  //... operation to run within the transaction ...
});
```

This is such a small step with a huge savings. The policy to check the status and update the audit trails is abstracted and encapsulated within the runWithinTransaction() method. To this method we send a piece of code that needs to run in the context of a transaction. We no longer have to worry about forgetting to perform the steps or about the exceptions being handled well. The policy-enforcing function takes care of all that.

We'll cover how to use lambda expressions to enforce such policies in Chapter 5, *Working with Resources*, on page 87.

Extending Policies

Policies seem to grow around us—beyond their being enforced, enterprise applications require ways to extend them. Based on some configuration information we may have to add or remove a series of operations that, in turn, may have to be processed before core logic in a module is executed. This is a common task in Java, but it requires much forethought and design.

The machinery for extensibility is often one or more interfaces. We could carefully design these interfaces and the hierarchy of classes that will implement them. The result may be effective, but this effort possibly leaves a number of interfaces and classes that we have to maintain. The design can easily become heavyweight and hard to maintain, jeopardizing the very goal of extensibility we set out for.

There's an alternative—functional interfaces and lambda expressions, which let us design extensible policies. This way we're not forced to create extra interfaces or conform to a method name, but instead we can focus on the core behaviors we'd like to provide, as we'll see in *Decorating Using Lambda Expressions*, on page 72.

Hassle-Free Concurrency

A big application is close to its delivery milestone when a huge performance issue comes to the surface. The team quickly figures out that the bottleneck is in the titanic module of the application, which involves processing large volumes of data. Someone on the team suggests that we can improve performance if we more effectively exploit the available multiple cores. But the excitement from the suggestion is likely short lived if the titanic module is like typical old-style Java code.

The team quickly realizes that converting the titanic module's code from a sequential to a concurrent version would take substantial effort, create additional complexity, and open doors for many multithreading-related bugs. Isn't there an easier way to get better performance?

What if there is no difference between sequential and concurrent code, and the effort to run it sequentially versus concurrently is merely the flip of a switch to clearly express our intent?

That may seem possible only in Narnia, but it's quite real if we develop our modules with functional purity. The internal iterators and functional style remove the last roadblock to easy parallelism. The JDK library has been designed to make the switch between serial and parallel execution require only a small and explicit but unobtrusive code change, as we'll see in *Taking a Leap to Parallelize*, on page 143.

Telling the Story

So much is lost in the translation between what the business wants and how the code implements it. The bigger that gap, the greater the chance of errors and higher the cost of maintenance. If the code reads more like the way the business states the problem, it becomes easier to read, easier to discuss with the business folks, and easier to evolve to meet their changing demands.

For instance, you hear the business say, "Get the prices for all the tickers, find the prices that are less than $500, and total the net asset value of only the stocks that make the cut." Using the new facilities available, we can write something like this:

```
tickers.map(StockUtil::getprice).filter(StockUtil::priceIsLessThan500).sum()
```

There's little chance of losing something in translation here, as there's not much to translate. This is function composition at work, and we'll see more of it in this book, especially in Chapter 8, *Composing with Lambda Expressions*, on page 135.

Separation of Concerns

A common need in applications is the separation of the core computations from the fine-grained logic the computations depend on. For example, an order-processing system may want to apply different tax computations based on the origin of transaction. Separating the tax-computation logic from the rest of the processing will help us create more reusable and extensible code.

In OOP we call this *separation of concern* and often use the strategy pattern to solve it. The effort typically involves creating one or more interfaces and a bunch of classes to implement them.

We can achieve the same now, but with far less code. And we can try out our design ideas really fast without being bogged down by a hierarchy of code that we have to lay out first. We'll cover how to create this pattern and separate concerns using lightweight functions in *Separating Concerns Using Lambda Expressions*, on page 63.

Delaying Evaluation

When creating enterprise applications, we may have to interact with web services, make database calls, process XML...the list goes on. There are so many operations that we have to perform, but not all of them are necessary all the time. Avoiding some operations or at least postponing the ones that don't have to be performed yet is one of the easiest ways to improve performance and application start-up or response time.

It's a simple goal, but one that may be quite hard to implement using a pure OOP approach. We would have to fuss with object references and null checks to postpone initialization of heavyweight objects, for instance.

Alternatively, we can minimize our effort and make the intent more explicit by using the new Optional class and the functional-style API it provides, as we'll see in *Delayed Initialization*, on page 103.

Improving Testability

Fewer things tend to break in code that has few moving parts. By nature, functional-style code is more resilient to change and requires relatively less testing effort.

In addition, as we'll see in Chapter 4, *Designing with Lambda Expressions*, on page 63, and Chapter 5, *Working with Resources*, on page 87, lambda expressions can stand in as lightweight mocks or stubs, and can help create highly expressive exception tests. Lambda expressions can also serve as a great testing aid. A common set of test cases can receive and exercise lambda expressions. The tests can capture the essence of behaviors that need to be tested for regression. At the same time, the lambda expressions being passed in can serve as variations of implementations that need to be exercised.

The automated tests that are part of the JDK itself are great examples of this —for more details browse through the JDK source code in the OpenJDK repository.[2]

These tests show how lambda expressions help parameterize the test cases' key behaviors; for example, they help compose the tests as "make a container for the results" followed by "assert some parameterized postconditions."

We've discussed how the functional style not only helps us write better quality code, but also solves elegantly so many of our common application development challenges. That means we can create applications more quickly, with

---

2. http://hg.openjdk.java.net

less effort and fewer errors—as long as we follow a few guidelines, as we'll discuss next.

Evolution, Not Revolution

To reap the benefits of functional style, we don't have to switch over to another language; we simply have to change the way we use Java.

Languages like C++, Java, and C# started out with support for imperative and object-oriented programming. Now all these languages also embrace the functional style of programming. We just saw examples of these two styles and discussed the benefits we derived from the functional style. Now let's look into some key concepts and practices that will help us adopt the new style.

The Java language team has put in substantial time and effort to bring functional capabilities to the language and the JDK. To reap the benefits, we have to pick up a few new concepts. We can improve our code if we follow some guidelines:

- Be declarative.
- Promote immutability.
- Avoid side effects.
- Prefer expressions over statements.
- Design with higher-order functions.

Let's quickly look at these practices.

Be Declarative

At the core of the familiar imperative style are mutability and command-driven programming. We create variables or objects and modify their state along the way. We also provide detailed commands or instructions to execute, such as create a loop index, increment its value, check if we reached the end, update the nth element of an array, and so on. It made sense for us to program this way in the past due to the nature of the tools and the hardware limitations.

We saw how the declarative use of the contains() method—when used on an immutable collection—was far easier to work with than the imperative style. All the hard work and the lower-level details were moved into the library function and we don't have to deal with those details. We would prefer doing everything this way if it were only easier. Immutability and declarative programming are the essence of the functional style of programming, and Java now makes them quite approachable.

Promote Immutability

Mutable code has many moving parts. The more things change, the easier it is for components to break and for errors to creep in. Code where multiple variables change is hard to understand and quite difficult to parallelize. Immutability removes all these problems at the root.

Java supports immutability but does not enforce it—but we can. We need to change our old habits of mutating objects' states. As much as possible, we must use immutable objects.

When declaring variables, fields, and parameters, lean toward declaring them final, following the sage advice "Treat objects as immutable" from *Effective Java [Blo08]*, by Joshua Bloch.

When creating objects, promote immutable objects such as the String class. When working with collections, create immutable or unmodifiable collections using functions like Arrays.asList() or the Collections class's unmodifiableList() method, for example.

By avoiding mutability we can create pure functions—that is, functions with no side effects.

Avoid Side Effects

Imagine writing a piece of code to go out to the Web to fetch a stock price and then update a shared variable. If we have a number of prices to fetch, we're forced to run these time-consuming operations sequentially. If we resort to multithreading, then we have to burden ourselves with threading and synchronization issues to prevent race conditions. The net result is poor application performance and/or lack of sleep trying to manage multiple threads. We can totally eliminate the problems by removing the side effect.

A function with no side effects honors immutability and does not change its input or anything in its reach. These functions are easier to understand, have fewer errors, and are easier to optimize. The lack of side effects removes any concerns of race conditions or simultaneous updates. As a result we can also easily parallelize execution of such functions, as we'll see in *Taking a Leap to Parallelize*, on page 143.

Prefer Expressions Over Statements

Statements are stubborn and force mutation. Expressions promote immutability and function composition. For example, we first used the for statement to compute the total of discounted prices. This version promoted mutation and verbose code. By switching over to the more expressive declarative version using the map() and sum() methods, which are expressions, we avoided mutations and were able to chain or compose functions.

It's better to design with expressions and use them more than statements in our code. This will now make the code concise and easier to understand. The code will flow logically, in the same order in which we would state the problem. The concise version is easier to change if the problem changes.

Design with Higher-Order Functions

Unlike some functional programming languages, such as Haskell, that enforce immutability, Java lets us modify variables at will. In that regard Java is not, and will never be, a pure functional programming language. However, we can write code in the functional style in Java by using higher-order functions.

A higher-order function takes the concept of reuse to the next level. Instead of solely relying on objects and classes to promote reuse, with higher-order functions we can easily reuse small, focused, cohesive, and well-written functions.

In OOP we're used to passing objects to methods, creating objects within methods, and returning objects from within methods. Higher-order functions do to functions what methods did to objects. With higher-order functions we can

- Pass functions to functions
- Create functions within functions
- Return functions from functions

We already saw an example of passing a function to another function, and we'll see examples of creating and returning functions later. Let's look at our "passing a function to a function" example again.

```
prices.stream()
      .filter(price -> price.compareTo(BigDecimal.valueOf(20)) > 0)
      .map(price -> price.multiply(BigDecimal.valueOf(0.9)))
      .reduce(BigDecimal.ZERO, BigDecimal::add);
```

In this example we're sending a function, price -> price.multiply(BigDecimal.valueOf(0.9)), as an argument to map. The function being passed is created just in time, at the point of call to the higher-order function map. Generally a function has a body, a name, a parameter list, and a return type. The just-in-time function created here has a parameter list followed by an arrow (->), and then the short body. The type of the parameter may be inferred by the Java compiler here and the return type is implicit. This function is anonymous; it has no name.

Rather than referring to these as anonymous functions, we call them *lambda expressions*.

Passing anonymous functions is not a totally unknown concept in Java; we're used to passing instances of anonymous classes. If our anonymous class had only one method, we still had to go through the ceremony of creating a class, albeit anonymous, and instantiating it. Instead we can now enjoy a lightweight syntax in Java with lambda expressions. Additionally, we're accustomed to abstracting concepts with objects. Now we can combine that with abstracting behavior using lambda expressions.

It takes some rethinking to design applications with this style of programming. We have to tune our imperative-ingrained minds to think functionally. This may seem a bit difficult at the beginning, but we'll get used to it in no time, and can leave those dysfunctional APIs far behind as we move forward.

Let's now switch gears and look at how Java handles lambda expressions. We're used to passing objects to methods, but now we can store functions and pass them around. Let's look at the magic behind how Java accepts a function as an argument.

A Little Sugar to Sweeten

We could implement all the ideas with what was already available in Java, but lambda expressions remove the ceremony and sweeten our efforts by adding a little syntax sugar. This quickly translates into code that's faster to create and makes it easier to express our ideas.

In the past we've used a number of interfaces that only have single methods: Runnable, Callable, Comparable, and so on. These interfaces are common in the JDK library and often appear where just a single function is expected. All these existing library methods that expect a single method interface can now accept lightweight functions, thanks to the brilliant syntax sugar provided though functional interfaces.

A functional interface is an interface with one abstract—unimplemented—method. Again think single-method interfaces like Runnable, Callable, Comparable, and so on, which all fit that definition. JDK 8 has more of these types of interfaces—Function, Predicate, Consumer, Supplier, and so on (for a summary of the starter set of functional interfaces see Appendix 1, *Starter Set of Functional Interfaces*, on page 155). A functional interface may also have zero or more static methods and default methods, which are implemented right within the interface.

We can mark a functional interface with the @FunctionalInterface annotation. The compiler does not require this annotation, but it is helpful to explicitly state the purpose that the interface serves. Furthermore, if we mark an interface with this annotation, the compiler will enforce the rules for the interface to qualify as a functional interface.

If a method takes a functional interface as a parameter, then we can pass the following:

- An anonymous inner class, the old-fashioned way (but why would we?)
- A lambda expression, like we did when we called the map() method
- A method or constructor reference (as we'll see later)

The compiler readily accepts a lambda expression or a method/constructor reference as an argument if the method's corresponding parameter is a reference to a functional interface.

When we pass a lambda expression to a method, the compiler will convert the lambda expression to an instance of the appropriate functional interface. This conversion is not a mere generation of an inner class in place. The synthesized method of this instance conforms to the abstract method of the functional interface that corresponds to the argument. For example, the map() method takes the functional interface Function<T, R> as its parameter. In a call to the map() method, the Java compiler synthesizes it, as the following figure shows.

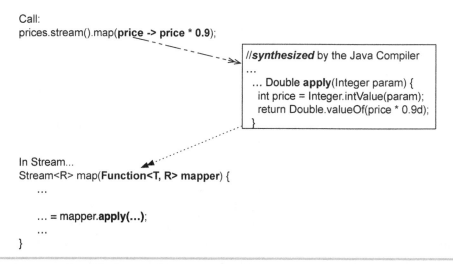

Call:
prices.stream().map(**price -> price * 0.9**);

//***synthesized*** by the Java Compiler
...
... Double **apply**(Integer param) {
int price = Integer.intValue(param);
return Double.valueOf(price * 0.9d);
}

In Stream...
Stream<R> map(**Function<T, R> mapper**) {
    ...

    ... = mapper.**apply(...)**;
    ...
}

Figure 2—Simplified view of the promotion from lambda expression to functional interface

The parameters of the lambda expression must match the parameters of the interface's abstract method. This synthesized method returns the lambda expression's result. If the return type doesn't directly match that of the abstract method, the synthesized method may convert the return value to a proper assignable type.

We took a peek at how lambda expressions are passed as arguments to methods. Let's quickly review what we covered and move on to explore lambda expressions.

Recap

It's a whole new world in Java. We can now program in an elegant and fluent functional style, with higher-order functions. This can lead to concise code that has fewer errors and is easier to understand, maintain, and parallelize. The Java compiler works its magic so we can send lambda expressions or method references where functional interfaces are expected.

We're all set to dive into the fun parts of lambda expressions and the JDK library that's been fine-tuned to work with lambda expressions. In the next chapter we'll start by using lambda expressions in one of the most fundamental programming tasks: working with collections.

If you cannot grok the overall structure of a program while taking a shower, you are not ready to code it.

➤ *Richard Pattis*

CHAPTER 2

Using Collections

We often use collections of numbers, strings, and objects. They are so commonplace that removing even a small amount of ceremony from coding collections can reduce code clutter greatly. In this chapter we explore the use of lambda expressions to manipulate collections. We use them to iterate collections, transform them into new collections, extract elements from them, and easily concatenate their elements.

After this chapter, our Java code to manipulate collections will never be the same—it'll be concise, expressive, elegant, and more extensible than ever before.

Iterating through a List

Iterating through a list is a basic operation on a collection, but over the years it's gone through a few significant changes. We'll begin with the old and evolve an example—enumerating a list of names—to the elegant style.

We can easily create an immutable collection of a list of names with the following code:

```
final List<String> friends =
  Arrays.asList("Brian", "Nate", "Neal", "Raju", "Sara", "Scott");
```

Here's the habitual, but not so desirable, way to iterate and print each of the elements.

collections/fpij/Iteration.java
```
for(int i = 0; i < friends.size(); i++) {
  System.out.println(friends.get(i));
}
```

I call this style *the self-inflicted wound pattern*—it's verbose and error prone. We have to stop and wonder, "is it i < or i <=?" This is useful only if we need to manipulate elements at a particular index in the collection, but even then, we can opt to use a functional style that favors immutability, as we'll discuss soon.

Java also offers a construct that is a bit more civilized than the good old for loop.

collections/fpij/Iteration.java
```
for(String name : friends) {
  System.out.println(name);
}
```

Under the hood this form of iteration uses the Iterator interface and calls into its hasNext() and next() methods.

Both these versions are *external iterators*, which mix *how* we do it with *what* we'd like to achieve. We explicitly control the iteration with them, indicating where to start and where to end; the second version does that under the hood using the Iterator methods. With explicit control, the break and continue statements can also help manage the iteration's flow of control.

The second construct has less ceremony than the first. Its style is better than the first if we don't intend to modify the collection at a particular index. Both of these styles, however, are imperative and we can dispense with them in modern Java.

There are quite a few reasons to favor the change to the functional style:

- The for loops are inherently sequential and are quite difficult to parallelize.

- Such loops are non-polymorphic; we get exactly what we ask for. We passed the collection to for instead of invoking a method (a polymorphic operation) on the collection to perform the task.

- At the design level, the code fails the "Tell, don't ask" principle. We ask for a specific iteration to be performed instead of leaving the details of the iteration to underlying libraries.

It's time to trade in the old imperative style for the more elegant functional-style version of *internal iteration*. With an internal iteration we willfully turn over most of the *how*s to the underlying library so we can focus on the essential *what*s. The underlying function will take care of managing the iteration. Let's use an internal iterator to enumerate the names.

The Iterable interface has been enhanced in JDK 8 with a special method named forEach(), which accepts a parameter of type Consumer. As the name indicates, an instance of Consumer will consume, through its accept() method, what's given to it. Let's use the forEach() method with the all-too-familiar anonymous inner class syntax.

collections/fpij/Iteration.java
```
friends.forEach(new Consumer<String>() {
  public void accept(final String name) {
    System.out.println(name);
  }
});
```

We invoked the forEach() on the friends collection and passed an anonymous instance of Consumer to it. The forEach() method will invoke the accept() method of the given Consumer for each element in the collection and let it do whatever it wants with it. In this example we merely print the given value, which is the name.

Let's look at the output from this version, which is the same as the output from the two previous versions:

```
Brian
Nate
Neal
Raju
Sara
Scott
```

We changed just one thing: we traded in the old for loop for the new internal iterator forEach(). As for the benefit, we went from specifying how to iterate to focusing on what we want to do for each element. The bad news is the code looks a lot more verbose—so much that it can drain away any excitement about the new style of programming. Thankfully, we can fix that quickly; this is where lambda expressions and the new compiler magic come in. Let's make one change again, replacing the anonymous inner class with a lambda expression.

collections/fpij/Iteration.java
```
friends.forEach((final String name) -> System.out.println(name));
```

That's a lot better. We look at less code, but watch closely to see what's in there. The forEach() is a higher-order function that accepts a lambda expression or block of code to execute in the context of each element in the list. The variable name is bound to each element of the collection during the call. The underlying library takes control of how the lambda expressions are evaluated. It can decide to perform them lazily, in any order, and exploit parallelism as it sees fit.

This version produces the same output as the previous versions.

The internal-iterator version is more concise than the other ones. However, when we use it we're able to focus our attention on what we want to achieve for each element rather than how to sequence through the iteration—it's declarative.

This version has a limitation, however. Once the forEach method starts, unlike in the other two versions, we can't break out of the iteration. (There are facilities to handle this limitation.) As a consequence, this style is useful in the common case where we want to process each element in a collection. Later we'll see alternate functions that give us control over the path of iteration.

The standard syntax for lambda expressions expects the parameters to be enclosed in parentheses, with the type information provided and comma separated. The Java compiler also offers some lenience and can infer the types. Leaving out the type is convenient, requires less effort, and is less noisy. Here's the previous code without the type information.

collections/fpij/Iteration.java
```
friends.forEach((name) -> System.out.println(name));
```

In this case, the Java compiler determines the name parameter's a String type, based on the context. It looks up the signature of the called method, forEach() in this example, and analyzes the functional interface it takes as a parameter. It then looks at that interface's abstract method to determine the expected number of parameters and their types. We can also use type inference if a lambda expression takes multiple parameters, but in that case we must leave out the type information for all the parameters; we have to specify the type for *none* or for *all* of the parameters in a lambda expression.

The Java compiler treats single-parameter lambda expressions as special: we can leave off the parentheses around the parameter if the parameter's type is inferred.

collections/fpij/Iteration.java
```
friends.forEach(name -> System.out.println(name));
```

There's one caveat: inferred parameters are non-final. In the previous example, where we explicitly specified the type, we also marked the parameter as final. This prevents us from modifying the parameter within the lambda expression. In general, modifying parameters is in poor taste and leads to errors, so marking them final is a good practice. Unfortunately, when we favor type inference we have to practice extra discipline not to modify the parameter, as the compiler will not protect us.

We have come a long way with this example and reduced the code quite a bit. But there's more. Let's take one last step to tease out another ounce of conciseness.

collections/fpij/Iteration.java
```
friends.forEach(System.out::println);
```

In the preceding code we used a *method reference*. Java lets us simply replace the body of code with the method name of our choice. We will dig into this further in the next section, but for now let's reflect on the wise words of Antoine de Saint-Exupéry: "Perfection is achieved not when there is nothing more to add, but when there is nothing left to take away."

Lambda expressions helped us concisely iterate over a collection. Next we'll cover how they help remove mutability and make the code even more concise when transforming collections.

Transforming a List

Manipulating a collection to produce another result is as easy as iterating through the elements of a collection. Suppose we're asked to convert a list of names to all capital letters. Let's explore some options to achieve this.

Java's String is immutable, so instances can't be changed. We could create new strings in all caps and replace the appropriate elements in the collection. However, the original collection would be lost; also, if the original list is immutable, like it is when created with Arrays.asList(), then the list can't change. Another downside is it would be hard to parallelize the computations.

Creating a new list that has the elements in all caps is a better option.

That suggestion may seem quite naive at first; performance is an obvious concern we all share. Surprisingly, the functional approach often yields better performance than the imperative approach, as we'll see in *Performance Concerns*, on page 151.

Let's start by creating a new collection of uppercase names from the given collection.

collections/fpij/Transform.java
```
final List<String> uppercaseNames = new ArrayList<String>();

for(String name : friends) {
  uppercaseNames.add(name.toUpperCase());
}
```

In this imperative style, we created an empty list then populated it with all-uppercase names, one element at a time, while iterating through the original list. As a first step to move toward a functional style, we could use the internal iterator forEach() method from *Iterating through a List*, on page 19, to replace the for loop, as we see next.

collections/fpij/Transform.java
```
final List<String> uppercaseNames = new ArrayList<String>();
friends.forEach(name -> uppercaseNames.add(name.toUpperCase()));
System.out.println(uppercaseNames);
```

We used the internal iterator, but that still required the empty list and the effort to add elements to it. We can do a lot better.

Using Lambda Expressions

The map() method of a new Stream interface can help us avoid mutability and make the code concise. A Stream is much like an iterator on a collection of objects and provides some nice *fluent functions*. Using the methods of this interface, we can compose a sequence of calls so that the code reads and flows in the same way we'd state problems, making it easier to read.

The Stream's map() method can map or transform a sequence of input to a sequence of output—that fits quite well for the task at hand.

collections/fpij/Transform.java
```
friends.stream()
        .map(name -> name.toUpperCase())
        .forEach(name -> System.out.print(name + " "));
System.out.println();
```

The method stream() is available on all collections in JDK 8 and it wraps the collection into an instance of Stream. The map() method applies the given lambda expression or block of code, within the parenthesis, on each element in the Stream. The map() method is quite unlike the forEach() method, which simply runs the block in the context of each element in the collection. In addition, the map() method collects the result of running the lambda expression and returns the result collection. Finally, we print the elements in this result using the forEach() method. The names in the new collection are in all caps:

BRIAN NATE NEAL RAJU SARA SCOTT

The map() method is quite useful to map or transform an input collection into a new output collection. This method will ensure that the same number of elements exists in the input and the output sequence. However, element types in the input don't have to match the element types in the output collection. In this example, both the input and the output are a collection of strings. We could have passed to the map() method a block of code that returned, for example, the number of characters in a given name. In this case, the input would still be a sequence of strings, but the output would be a sequence of numbers, as in the next example.

collections/fpij/Transform.java

```
friends.stream()
       .map(name -> name.length())
       .forEach(count -> System.out.print(count + " "));
```

The result is a count of the number of letters in each name:

```
5 4 4 4 4 5
```

The versions using the lambda expressions have no explicit mutation; they're concise. These versions also didn't need any initial empty collection or garbage variable; that variable quietly receded into the shadows of the underlying implementation.

Using Method References

We can nudge the code to be just a bit more concise by using a feature called *method reference*. The Java compiler will take either a lambda expression or a reference to a method where an implementation of a functional interface is expected. With this feature, a short String::toUpperCase can replace name -> name.toUpperCase(), like so:

collections/fpij/Transform.java

```
friends.stream()
       .map(String::toUpperCase)
       .forEach(name -> System.out.println(name));
```

Java knows to invoke the String class's given method toUpperCase() on the parameter passed in to the synthesized method—the implementation of the functional interface's abstract method. That parameter reference is implicit here. In simple situations like the previous example, we can substitute method references for lambda expressions; see *When should we use method references?*, on page 26.

In the preceding example, the method reference was for an instance method. Method references can also refer to static methods and methods that take parameters. We'll see examples of these later.

Lambda expressions helped us enumerate a collection and transform it into a new collection. They can also help us concisely pick an element from a collection, as we'll see next.

> ### Joe asks:
> ### When should we use method references?
>
> We'd normally use lambda expressions much more than method references when programming in Java. That doesn't mean method references are unimportant or less useful, though. They are nice replacements when the lambda expressions are really short and make simple, direct calls to either an instance method or a static method. In other words, if lambda expressions merely pass their parameters through, we can replace them with method references.
>
> These candidate lambda expressions are much like Tom Smykowski, in the movie *Office Space*,[a] whose job is to "take specifications from the customers and bring them down to the software engineers." For this reason, I call the refactoring of lambdas to method references *the office-space pattern*.
>
> In addition to conciseness, by using method references we gain the ability to use more directly the names already chosen for these methods.
>
> There's quite a bit of compiler magic under the hood when we use method references. The method reference's target object and parameters are derived from the parameters passed to the synthesized method. This makes the code with method references much more concise than the code with lambda expressions. However, we can't use this convenience if we have to manipulate parameters before sending them as arguments or tinker with the call's results before returning them.
>
> _____
> a.   http://en.wikipedia.org/wiki/Office_Space

Finding Elements

The now-familiar elegant methods to traverse and transform collections will not directly help pick elements from a collection. The filter() method is designed for that purpose.

From a list of names, let's pick the ones that start with the letter *N*. Since there may be zero matching names in the list, the result may be an empty list. Let's first code it using the old approach.

```
collections/fpij/PickElements.java
final List<String> startsWithN = new ArrayList<String>();
for(String name : friends) {
  if(name.startsWith("N")) {
    startsWithN.add(name);
  }
}
```

That's a chatty piece of code for a simple task. We created a variable and initialized it to an empty collection. Then we looped through the collection, looking for a name that starts with the desired letter. If found, we added the element to the collection.

Let's refactor this code to use the filter() method, and see how it changes things.

collections/fpij/PickElements.java

```
final List<String> startsWithN =
  friends.stream()
        .filter(name -> name.startsWith("N"))
        .collect(Collectors.toList());
```

The filter() method expects a lambda expression that returns a boolean result. If the lambda expression returns a true, the element in context while executing that lambda expression is added to a result collection; it's skipped otherwise. Finally the method returns a Stream with only elements for which the lambda expression yielded a true. In the end we transformed the result into a List using the collect() method—we'll discuss this method further in *Using the collect Method and the Collectors Class*, on page 52.

Let's print the number of elements in the result collection.

collections/fpij/PickElements.java

```
System.out.println(String.format("Found %d names", startsWithN.size()));
```

From the output it's clear that the method picked up the proper number of elements from the input collection.

```
Found 2 names
```

The filter() method returns an iterator just like the map() method does, but the similarity ends there. Whereas the map() method returns a collection of the same size as the input collection, the filter() method may not. It may yield a result collection with a number of elements ranging from zero to the maximum number of elements in the input collection. However, unlike map(), the elements in the result collection that filter() returned are a subset of the elements in the input collection.

The conciseness we've achieved by using lambda expressions so far is nice, but code duplication may sneak in quickly if we're not careful. Let's address that concern next.

Reusing Lambda Expressions

Lambda expressions are deceivingly concise and it's easy to carelessly duplicate them in code. Duplicate code leads to poor-quality code that's hard to maintain; if we needed to make a change, we'd have to find and touch the relevant code in several places.

Avoiding duplication can also help improve performance. By keeping the code related to a piece of knowledge concentrated in one place, we can easily study its performance profile and make changes in one place to get better performance.

Now let's see how easy it is to fall into the duplication trap when using lambda expressions, and consider ways to avoid it.

Suppose we have a few collections of names: friends, editors, comrades, and so on.

```
final List<String> friends =
  Arrays.asList("Brian", "Nate", "Neal", "Raju", "Sara", "Scott");

final List<String> editors =
  Arrays.asList("Brian", "Jackie", "John", "Mike");

final List<String> comrades =
  Arrays.asList("Kate", "Ken", "Nick", "Paula", "Zach");
```

We want to filter out names that start with a certain letter. Let's first take a naive approach to this using the filter() method.

collections/fpij/PickElementsMultipleCollection.java
```
final long countFriendsStartN =
  friends.stream()
        .filter(name -> name.startsWith("N")).count();

final long countEditorsStartN =
  editors.stream()
        .filter(name -> name.startsWith("N")).count();

final long countComradesStartN =
  comrades.stream()
        .filter(name -> name.startsWith("N")).count();
```

The lambda expressions made the code concise, but quietly led to duplicate code. In the previous example, one change to the lambda expression needs to change in more than one place—that's a *no-no*. Fortunately, we can assign lambda expressions to variables and reuse them, just like with objects.

The filter() method, the receiver of the lambda expression in the previous example, takes a reference to a java.util.function.Predicate functional interface. Here, the Java compiler works its magic to synthesize an implementation of the Predicate's test() method from the given lambda expression. Rather than asking Java to synthesize the method at the argument-definition location, we can be more explicit. In this example, it's possible to store the lambda expression in an explicit reference of type Predicate and then pass it to the function; this is an easy way to remove the duplication.

Let's refactor the previous code to make it DRY.[1] (See the Don't Repeat Yourself —DRY—principle in *The Pragmatic Programmer: From Journeyman to Master* *[HT00]*, by Andy Hunt and Dave Thomas.)

```
collections/fpij/PickElementsMultipleCollection.java
final Predicate<String> startsWithN = name -> name.startsWith("N");

final long countFriendsStartN =
  friends.stream()
        .filter(startsWithN)
        .count();
final long countEditorsStartN =
  editors.stream()
        .filter(startsWithN)
        .count();
final long countComradesStartN =
  comrades.stream()
         .filter(startsWithN)
         .count();
```

Rather than duplicate the lambda expression several times, we created it once and stored it in a reference named startsWithN of type Predicate. In the three calls to the filter() method, the Java compiler happily took the lambda expression stored in the variable under the guise of the Predicate instance.

The new variable gently removed the duplication that sneaked in. Unfortunately, it's about to sneak back in with a vengeance, as we'll see next, and we need something a bit more powerful to thwart it.

Using Lexical Scoping and Closures

There's a misconception among some developers that using lambda expressions may introduce duplication and lower code quality. Contrary to that belief, even when the code gets more complicated we still don't need to compromise code quality to enjoy the conciseness that lambda expressions give, as we'll see in this section.

We managed to reuse the lambda expression in the previous example; however, duplication will sneak in quickly when we bring in another letter to match. Let's explore the problem further and then solve it using lexical scoping and closures.

---

1. http://c2.com/cgi/wiki?DontRepeatYourself

Duplication in Lambda Expressions

Let's pick the names that start with *N* or *B* from the friends collection of names. Continuing with the previous example, we may be tempted to write something like the following:

```
collections/fpij/PickDifferentNames.java
final Predicate<String> startsWithN = name -> name.startsWith("N");
final Predicate<String> startsWithB = name -> name.startsWith("B");

final long countFriendsStartN =
  friends.stream()
        .filter(startsWithN).count();
final long countFriendsStartB =
  friends.stream()
        .filter(startsWithB).count();
```

The first predicate tests if the name starts with an *N* and the second tests for a *B*. We pass these two instances to the two calls to the filter() method, respectively. Seems reasonable, but the two predicates are mere duplicates, with only the letter they use being different. Let's figure out a way to eliminate this duplication.

Removing Duplication with Lexical Scoping

As a first option, we could extract the letter as a parameter to a function and pass the function as an argument to the filter() method. That's a reasonable idea, but the filter() method will not accept some arbitrary function. It insists on receiving a function that accepts one parameter representing the context element in the collection, and returning a boolean result. It's expecting a Predicate.

For comparison purposes we need a variable that will cache the letter for later use, and hold onto it until the parameter, name in this example, is received. Let's create a function for that.

```
collections/fpij/PickDifferentNames.java
public static Predicate<String> checkIfStartsWith(final String letter) {
  return name -> name.startsWith(letter);
}
```

We defined checkIfStartsWith() as a static function that takes a letter of type String as a parameter. It then returns a Predicate that can be passed to the filter() method for later evaluation. Unlike the higher-order functions we've seen so far, which accepted functions as parameters, the checkIfStartsWith() returns a function as a result. This is also a higher-order function, as we discussed in *Evolution, Not Revolution*, on page 12.

The Predicate that checkIfStartsWith() returned is different from the lambda expressions we've seen so far. In return name -> name.startsWith(letter), it's clear what name is: it's the parameter passed to this lambda expression. But what's the variable letter bound to? Since that's not in the scope of this anonymous function, Java reaches over to the scope of the definition of this lambda expression and finds the variable letter in that scope. This is called *lexical scoping*. Lexical scoping is a powerful technique that lets us cache values provided in one context for use later in another context. Since this lambda expression *closes over* the scope of its definition, it's also referred to as a *closure*. For lexical scope access restriction, see *Are there restrictions to lexical scoping?*, on page 31.

 Joe asks:
Are there restrictions to lexical scoping?

From within a lambda expression we can only access local variables that are final or *effectively* final in the enclosing scope.

A lambda expression may be invoked right away, or it may be invoked lazily or from multiple threads. To avoid race conditions, the local variables we access in the enclosing scope are not allowed to change once initialized. Any attempt to change them will result in a compilation error.

Variables marked final directly fit this bill, but Java does not insist that we mark them as such. Instead, Java looks for two things. First, the accessed variables have to be initialized within the enclosing methods before the lambda expression is defined. Second, the values of these variables don't change anywhere else—that is, they're effectively final although they are not marked as such.

When using lambda expressions that capture local state, we should be aware that stateless lambda expressions are runtime constants, but those that capture local state have an additional evaluation cost.

We can use the lambda expression returned by checkIfStartsWith() in the call to the filter() method, like so:

collections/fpij/PickDifferentNames.java
```
final long countFriendsStartN =
  friends.stream()
        .filter(checkIfStartsWith("N")).count();
final long countFriendsStartB =
  friends.stream()
        .filter(checkIfStartsWith("B")).count();
```

In the calls to the filter() method, we first invoke the checkIfStartsWith() method, passing in a desired letter. This call immediately returns a lambda expression that is then passed on to the filter() method.

By creating a higher-order function, checkIfStartsWith() in this example, and using lexical scoping, we managed to remove the duplication in code. We did not have to repeat the comparison to check if the name starts with different letters.

Refactoring to Narrow the Scope

In the preceding (smelly) example we used a static method, but we don't want to pollute the class with static methods to cache each variable in the future. It would be nice to narrow the function's scope to where it's needed. We can do that using a Function interface.

collections/fpij/PickDifferentNames.java

```
final Function<String, Predicate<String>> startsWithLetter =
  (String letter) -> {
    Predicate<String> checkStarts = (String name) -> name.startsWith(letter);
    return checkStarts;
};
```

This lambda expression replaces the static method checkIfStartsWith() and can appear within a function, just before it's needed. The startsWithLetter variable refers to a Function that takes in a String and returns a Predicate.

This version is verbose compared to the static method we saw earlier, but we'll refactor that soon to make it concise. For all practical purposes, this function is equivalent to the static method; it takes a String and returns a Predicate. Instead of explicitly creating the instance of the Predicate and returning it, we can replace it with a lambda expression.

collections/fpij/PickDifferentNames.java

```
final Function<String, Predicate<String>> startsWithLetter =
  (String letter) -> (String name) -> name.startsWith(letter);
```

We reduced clutter, but we can take the conciseness up another notch by removing the types and letting the Java compiler infer the types based on the context. Let's look at the concise version.

collections/fpij/PickDifferentNames.java

```
final Function<String, Predicate<String>> startsWithLetter =
  letter -> name -> name.startsWith(letter);
```

It takes a bit of effort to get used to this concise syntax. Feel free to look away for a moment if this makes you cross-eyed. Now that we've refactored that version, we can use it in place of the checkIfStartsWith(), like so:

```
collections/fpij/PickDifferentNames.java
final long countFriendsStartN =
  friends.stream()
        .filter(startsWithLetter.apply("N")).count();
final long countFriendsStartB =
  friends.stream()
        .filter(startsWithLetter.apply("B")).count();
```

We've come full circle with higher-order functions in this section. Our examples illustrate how to pass functions to functions, create functions within functions, and return functions from within functions. They also demonstrate the conciseness and reusability that lambda expressions facilitate.

We made good use of both Function and Predicate in this section, but let's discuss how they're different. A Predicate<T> takes in one parameter of type T and returns a boolean result to indicate a decision for whatever check it represents. We can use it anytime we want to make a go or no-go decision for a candidate we pass to the predicate. Methods like filter() that evaluate candidate elements take in a Predicate as their parameters. On the other hand, a Function<T, R> represents a function that takes a parameter of type T and returns a result of type R. This is more general than a Predicate that always returns a boolean. We can use a Function anywhere we want to transform an input to another value, so it's quite logical that the map() method uses Function as its parameter.

Selecting elements from a collection was easy. Next we'll cover how to pick just one element out of a collection.

Picking an Element

It's reasonable to expect that picking one element from a collection would be simpler than picking multiple elements. But there are a few complications. Let's look at the complexity introduced by the habitual approach and then bring in lambda expressions to solve it.

Let's create a method that will look for an element that starts with a given letter, and print it.

```
collections/fpij/PickAnElement.java
public static void pickName(
  final List<String> names, final String startingLetter) {
  String foundName = null;
  for(String name : names) {
    if(name.startsWith(startingLetter)) {
      foundName = name;
      break;
    }
  }
```

```
      System.out.print(String.format("A name starting with %s: ", startingLetter));

    if(foundName != null) {
      System.out.println(foundName);
    } else {
      System.out.println("No name found");
    }
}
```

This method's odor can easily compete with passing garbage trucks. We first created a foundName variable and initialized it to null—that's the source of our first bad smell. This will force a null check, and if we forget to deal with it the result could be a NullPointerException or an unpleasant response. We then used an external iterator to loop through the elements, but had to break out of the loop if we found an element—here are other sources of rancid smells: primitive obsession, imperative style, and mutability. Once out of the loop, we had to check the response and print the appropriate result. That's quite a bit of code for a simple task.

Let's rethink the problem. We simply want to pick the first matching element and safely deal with the absence of such an element. Let's rewrite the pickName() method, this time using lambda expressions.

collections/fpij/PickAnElementElegant.java
```
public static void pickName(
  final List<String> names, final String startingLetter) {

  final Optional<String> foundName =
    names.stream()
        .filter(name ->name.startsWith(startingLetter))
        .findFirst();

  System.out.println(String.format("A name starting with %s: %s",
    startingLetter, foundName.orElse("No name found")));
}
```

Some powerful features in the JDK library came together to help achieve this conciseness. First we used the filter() method to grab all the elements matching the desired pattern. Then the findFirst() method of the Stream class helped pick the first value from that collection. This method returns a special Optional object, which is the state-appointed null deodorizer in Java.

The Optional class is useful whenever the result may be absent. It protects us from getting a NullPointerException by accident and makes it quite explicit to the reader that "no result found" is a possible outcome. We can inquire if an object is present by using the isPresent() method, and we can obtain the current value using its get() method. Alternatively, we could suggest a substitute value for the missing instance, using the method (with the most threatening name) orElse(), like in the previous code.

Let's exercise the pickName() function with the sample friends collection we've used in the examples so far.

collections/fpij/PickAnElementElegant.java
```
pickName(friends, "N");
pickName(friends, "Z");
```

The code picks out the first matching element, if found, and prints an appropriate message otherwise.

```
A name starting with N: Nate
A name starting with Z: No name found
```

The combination of the findFirst() method and the Optional class reduced our code and its smell quite a bit. We're not limited to the preceding options when working with Optional, though. For example, rather than providing an alternate value for the absent instance, we can ask Optional to run a block of code or a lambda expression only if a value is present, like so:

collections/fpij/PickAnElementElegant.java
```
foundName.ifPresent(name -> System.out.println("Hello " + name));
```

When compared to using the imperative version to pick the first matching name, the nice, flowing functional style looks better. But are we doing more work in the fluent version than we did in the imperative version? The answer is no—these methods have the smarts to perform only as much work as is necessary (we'll talk about this more in *Leveraging the Laziness of Streams*, on page 111).

The search for the first matching element demonstrated a few more neat capabilities in the JDK. Next we'll look at how lambda expressions help compute a single result from a collection.

Reducing a Collection to a Single Value

We've gone over quite a few techniques to manipulate collections so far: picking matching elements, selecting a particular element, and transforming a collection. All these operations have one thing in common: they all worked independently on individual elements in the collection. None required comparing elements against each other or carrying over computations from one element to the next. In this section we look at how to compare elements and carry over a computational state across a collection.

Let's start with some basic operations and build up to something a bit more sophisticated. As the first example, let's read over the values in the friends collection of names and determine the total number of characters.

collections/fpij/PickALongest.java

```
System.out.println("Total number of characters in all names: " +
  friends.stream()
          .mapToInt(name -> name.length())
          .sum());
```

To find the total of the characters we need the length of each name. We can easily compute that using the mapToInt() method. Once we transform from the names to their lengths, the final step is to total them. This step we perform using the built-in sum() method. Here's the output for this operation:

```
Total number of characters in all names: 26
```

We leveraged the mapToInt() method, a variation of the *map* operation (variations like mapToInt(), mapToDouble(), and so on create type-specialized streams such as IntStream and DoubleStream) and then *reduced* the resulting length to the sum value.

Instead of using the sum() method, we could use a variety of methods like max() to find the longest length, min() to find the shortest length, sorted() to sort the lengths, average() to find the average of the length, and so on.

The hidden charm in the preceding example is the increasingly popular *MapReduce* pattern,[2] with the map() method being the spread operation and the sum() method being the special case of the more general reduce operation. In fact, the implementation of the sum() method in the JDK uses a reduce() method. Let's look at the more general form of reduce.

As an example, let's read over the given collection of names and display the longest one. If there is more than one name with the same longest length, we'll display the first one we find. One way we could do that is to figure out the longest length, and then pick the first element of that length. But that'd require going over the list twice—not efficient. This is where a reduce() method comes into play.

We can use the reduce() method to compare two elements against each other and pass along the result for further comparison with the remaining elements in the collection. Much like the other higher-order functions on collections we've seen so far, the reduce() method iterates over the collection. In addition,

---

2. http://research.google.com/archive/mapreduce.html

it carries forward the result of the computation that the lambda expression returned. An example will help clarify this, so let's get down to the code.

```
collections/fpij/PickALongest.java
final Optional<String> aLongName =
  friends.stream()
         .reduce((name1, name2) ->
             name1.length() >= name2.length() ? name1 : name2);
aLongName.ifPresent(name ->
  System.out.println(String.format("A longest name: %s", name)));
```

The lambda expression we're passing to the reduce() method takes two parameters, name1 and name2, and returns one of them based on the length. The reduce() method has no clue about our specific intent. That concern is separated from this method into the lambda expression that we pass to it— this is a lightweight application of the *strategy pattern*.[3]

This lambda expression conforms to the interface of an apply() method of a JDK functional interface named BinaryOperator. This is the type of the parameter the reduce() method receives. Let's run the reduce() method and see if it picks the first of the two longest names from our friends list.

```
A longest name: Brian
```

As the reduce() method iterated through the collection, it called the lambda expression first, with the first two elements in the list. The result from the lambda expression is used for the subsequent call. In the second call name1 is bound to the result from the previous call to the lambda expression, and name2 is bound to the third element in the collection. The calls to the lambda expression continue for the rest of the elements in the collection. The result from the final call is returned as the result of the reduce() method call.

The result of the reduce() method is an Optional because the list on which reduce() is called may be empty. In that case, there would be no longest name. If the list had only one element, then reduce() would return that element and the lambda expression we pass would not be invoked.

From the example we can infer that the reduce() method's result is at most one element from the collection. If we want to set a default or a base value, we can pass that value as an extra parameter to an overloaded variation of the reduce() method. For example, if the shortest name we want to pick is Steve, we can pass that to the reduce() method, like so:

---

3. See *Design Patterns: Elements of Reusable Object-Oriented Software [GHJV95]*, by Gamma et al.

collections/fpij/PickALongest.java

```
final String steveOrLonger =
  friends.stream()
        .reduce("Steve", (name1, name2) ->
          name1.length() >= name2.length() ? name1 : name2);
```

If any name was longer than the given base, it would get picked up; otherwise the function would return the base value, Steve in this example. This version of reduce() does not return an Optional since if the collection is empty, the default will be returned; there's no concern of an absent or nonexistent value.

Before we wrap up this chapter, let's visit a fundamental yet seemingly difficult operation on collections: joining elements.

Joining Elements

We've explored how to select elements, iterate, and transform collections. Yet in a trivial operation—concatenating a collection—we could lose all the gains we made with concise and elegant code if not for a newly added join() function. This simple method is so useful that it's poised to become one of the most used functions in the JDK. Let's see how to use it to print the values in a list, comma separated.

Let's work with our friends list. What does it take to print the list of names, separated by commas, using only the old JDK libraries?

We have to iterate through the list and print each element. Since the Java 5 for construct is better than the archaic for loop, let's start with that.

collections/fpij/PrintList.java

```
for(String name : friends) {
  System.out.print(name + ", ");
}
System.out.println();
```

That was simple code, but let's look at what it yielded.

```
Brian, Nate, Neal, Raju, Sara, Scott,
```

Darn it; there's a stinking comma at the end (shall we blame it on Scott?). How do we tell Java not to place a comma there? Unfortunately, the loop will run its course and there's no easy way to tell the last element apart from the rest. To fix this, we can fall back on the habitual loop.

collections/fpij/PrintList.java

```
for(int i = 0; i < friends.size() - 1; i++) {
  System.out.print(friends.get(i) + ", ");
}
```

```
if(friends.size() > 0)
  System.out.println(friends.get(friends.size() - 1));
```

Let's see if the output of this version was decent.

```
Brian, Nate, Neal, Raju, Sara, Scott
```

The result looks good, but the code to produce the output does not. Beam us up, modern Java.

We no longer have to endure that pain. A StringJoiner class cleans up all that mess in Java 8 and the String class has an added convenience method join() to turn that smelly code into a simple one-liner.

collections/fpij/PrintList.java
```
System.out.println(String.join(", ", friends));
```

Let's quickly verify the output is as charming as the code that produced it.

```
Brian, Nate, Neal, Raju, Sara, Scott
```

Under the hood the String's join() method calls upon the StringJoiner to concatenate the values in the second argument, a varargs, into a larger string separated by the first argument. We're not limited to concatenating only with a comma using this feature. We could, for example, take a bunch of paths and concatenate them to form a classpath easily, thanks to the new methods and classes.

We saw how to join a list of elements; we can also transform the elements before joining them. We already know how to transform elements using the map() method. We can also be selective about which element we want to keep by using methods like filter(). The final step of joining the elements, separated by commas or something else, is simply a reduce operation.

We could use the reduce() method to concatenate elements into a string, but that would require some effort on our part. The JDK has a convenience method named collect(), which is another form of reduce that can help us collect values into a target destination.

The collect() method does the reduction but delegates the actual implementation or target to a collector. We could drop the transformed elements into an ArrayList, for instance. Or, to continue with the current example, we could collect the transformed elements into a string concatenated with commas.

collections/fpij/PrintList.java
```
System.out.println(
  friends.stream()
        .map(String::toUpperCase)
        .collect(joining(", ")));
```

We invoked the collect() on the transformed list and provided it a collector returned by the joining() method, which is a static method on a Collectors utility class. A collector acts as a sink object to receive elements passed by the collect() method and stores it in a desired format: ArrayList, String, and so on. We will explore the collect() method further in *Using the collect Method and the Collectors Class*, on page 52.

Here are the names, now in uppercase and comma separated.

```
BRIAN, NATE, NEAL, RAJU, SARA, SCOTT
```

The StringJoiner gives a lot more control over the format of concatenation; we can specify a prefix, a suffix, and infix character sequences, if we desire.

We saw how lambda expressions and the newly added classes and methods make programming in Java so much easier, and more fun too. Let's go over what we covered in this chapter.

Recap

Collections are commonplace in programming and, thanks to lambda expressions, using them is now much easier and simpler in Java. We can trade the longwinded old methods for elegant, concise code to perform the common operations on collections. Internal iterators make it convenient to traverse collections, transform collections without enduring mutability, and select elements from collections without much effort. Using these functions means less code to write. That can lead to more maintainable code, more code that does useful domain- or application-related logic, and less code to handle the basics of coding.

In the next chapter we'll cover how lambda expressions simplify another fundamental programming task: working with strings and comparing objects.

Make everything as simple as possible, but not simpler.

> Albert Einstein

CHAPTER 3

Strings, Comparators, and Filters

The JDK has evolved to include convenience methods that promote the functional style. When using familiar classes and interfaces from the library —String, for example—we need to look for opportunities to use these newer functions in place of the old style. Also, anywhere we used an anonymous inner class with just one method, we can now use lambda expressions to reduce clutter and ceremony.

In this chapter we'll use lambda expressions and method references to iterate over a String, to implement Comparators, to list files in a directory, and to observe file and directory changes. Quite a few methods introduced in the previous chapter will appear here again to help with the tasks at hand. Techniques you pick up along the way will help turn long, mundane tasks into concise code snippets you can quickly write and easily maintain.

Iterating a String

The chars() method is a new one in the String class from the CharSequence interface. It's useful for fluently iterating over the String's characters. We can use this convenient internal iterator to apply an operation on the individual characters that make up the string. Let's use it in an example to process a string. Along the way we'll discuss a few more handy ways to use method references.

compare/fpij/IterateString.java
```
final String str = "w00t";

str.chars()
   .forEach(ch -> System.out.println(ch));
```

The chars() method returns a Stream over which we can iterate, using the forEach() internal iterator. We get direct read access to the characters in the String within the iterator. Here's the result when we iterate and print each character.

119
48
48
116

The result is not quite what we'd expect. Instead of seeing letters we're seeing numbers. That's because the chars() method returns a stream of Integers representing the letters instead of a stream of Characters. Let's explore the API a bit further before we fix the output.

In the previous code we created a lambda expression in the argument list for the forEach() method. The implementation was a simple call where we routed the parameter directly as an argument to the println() method. Since this is a trivial operation, we can eliminate this mundane code with the help of the Java compiler. We can rely on it to do this parameter routing for us, using a method reference like we did in *Using Method References*, on page 25.

We already saw how to create a method reference for an instance method. For example, for the call name.toUpperCase(), the method reference is String::toUpperCase. In this example, however, we have a call on a static reference System.out. We can use either a class name or an expression to the left of the double colon in method references. Using this flexibility, it's quite easy to provide a reference to the println() method, as we see next.

compare/fpij/IterateString.java
```
str.chars()
    .forEach(System.out::println);
```

In this example we see the smarts of the Java compiler for parameter routing. Recall that lambda expressions and method references may stand in where implementations of functional interfaces are expected, and the Java compiler synthesizes the appropriate method in place (see *A Little Sugar to Sweeten*, on page 15). In the earlier method reference we used, String::toUppercase, the parameter to the synthesized method turned into the target of the method call, like so: parameter.toUppercase();. That's because the method reference is based on a class name (String). In this example, the method reference, again to an instance method, is based on an expression—an instance of PrintStream accessed through the static reference System.out. Since we already provided a target for the method, the Java compiler decided to use the parameter of the synthesized method as an argument to the referenced method, like so: System.out.println(parameter);. Sweet.

The code with the method reference is quite concise, but we have to dig into it a bit more to understand what's going on. Once we get used to method references, our brains will know to autoparse these.

In this example, although the code is concise, the output is not satisfactory. We want to see letters and not numbers in their place. To fix that, let's write a convenience method that prints an int as a letter.

compare/fpij/IterateString.java
```
private static void printChar(int aChar) {
  System.out.println((char)(aChar));
}
```

We can use a reference to this convenience method to fix the output.

compare/fpij/IterateString.java
```
str.chars()
   .forEach(IterateString::printChar);
```

We can continue to use the result of chars() as an int, and when it's time to print we can convert it to a character. The output of this version will display letters.

```
w
o
o
t
```

If we want to process characters and not int from the start, we can convert the ints to characters right after the call to the chars() method, like so:

compare/fpij/IterateString.java
```
str.chars()
   .mapToObj(ch -> Character.valueOf((char)ch))
   .forEach(System.out::println);
```

We used the internal iterator on the Stream that the chars() method returned, but we're not limited to that method. Once we get a Stream we can use any methods available on it, like map(), filter(), reduce(), and so on, to process the characters in the string. For example, we can filter out only digits from the string, like so:

compare/fpij/IterateString.java
```
str.chars()
   .filter(ch -> Character.isDigit(ch))
   .forEach(ch -> printChar(ch));
```

We can see the filtered digits in the next output.

```
0
0
```

Once again, instead of the lambda expressions we passed to the filter() method and the forEach() method, we can use references to the respective methods.

`compare/fpij/IterateString.java`
```
str.chars()
    .filter(Character::isDigit)
    .forEach(IterateString::printChar);
```

The method references here helped remove the mundane parameter routing. In addition, in this example we see yet another variation of method references compared to the previous two instances where we used them. When we first saw method references, we created one for an instance method. Later we created one for a call on a static reference. Now we're creating a method reference for a static method—method references seem to keep on giving.

The one for an instance method and the one for a static method look the same structurally: for example, String::toUppercase and Character::isDigit. To decide how to route the parameter, the Java compiler will check whether the method is an instance method or a static method. If it's an instance method, then the synthesized method's parameter becomes the call's target, like in parameter.toUppercase(); (the exception to this rule is if the target is already specified like in System.out::println). On the other hand, if the method is static, then the parameter to the synthesized method is routed as an argument to this method, like in Character.isDigit(parameter);. See Appendix 2, *Syntax Overview*, on page 157, for a listing of method-reference variations and their syntax.

While this parameter routing is quite convenient, there is one caveat—method collisions and the resulting ambiguity. If there's both a matching instance method and a static method, we'll get a compilation error due to the reference's ambiguity. For example, if we write Double::toString to convert an instance of Double to a String, the compiler would get confused whether to use the public String toString() instance method or the static method public static String toString(double value), both from the Double class. If we run into this, no sweat; we simply switch back to using the appropriate lambda-expression version to move on.

Once we get used to the functional style, we can switch between the lambda expressions and the more concise method references, based on our comfort level.

We used a new method in Java 8 to easily iterate over characters. Next we'll explore the enhancements to the Comparator interface.

Implementing the Comparator Interface

The Comparator interface is used in hundreds of places in the JDK library, from searching operations to sorting, reversing, and so on. In Java 8 this has turned into a functional interface; the benefit is that we can use charmingly fluent syntax to implement comparators.

Let's create a few different implementations of the Comparator to understand the influence of the new style. Our fingers will thank us for all the keystrokes saved by not having to create anonymous inner classes.

Sorting with a Comparator

We'll build an example to sort a list of people using a few different points of comparisons. Let's first create the Person JavaBean.

```
compare/fpij/Person.java
public class Person {
  private final String name;
  private final int age;

  public Person(final String theName, final int theAge) {
    name = theName;
    age = theAge;
  }

  public String getName() { return name; }
  public int getAge() { return age; }

  public int ageDifference(final Person other) {
    return age - other.age;
  }

  public String toString() {
    return String.format("%s - %d", name, age);
  }
}
```

We could implement the Comparable interface on the Person class, but that'd limit us to one particular comparison. We would want to compare on different things—on name, age, or a combination of fields, for example. To get this flexibility, we'll create the code for different comparisons just when we need them, with the help of the Comparator interface.

Let's create a list of people to work with, folks with different names and ages.

```
compare/fpij/Compare.java
final List<Person> people = Arrays.asList(
  new Person("John", 20),
  new Person("Sara", 21),
  new Person("Jane", 21),
  new Person("Greg", 35));
```

We could sort the people by their names or ages and in ascending or descending order. In the habitual way to achieve this we would implement the Comparator interface using anonymous inner classes. But the essence here is the code for the comparison logic, and anything else we write would be pure ceremony. We can boil this down to its essence using lambda expressions.

Let's first sort the people in the list in ascending order by age.

Since we have a List, the obvious choice is the sort() method on the List. There are downsides to using this method, however. That's a void method, which means the list will be mutated when we call it. To preserve the original list, we'd have to make a copy and then invoke the sort() method on the copy; that's quite labor intensive. Instead we'll seek the help of the Stream.

We can get a Stream from the List and conveniently call the sorted() method on it. Rather than messing with the given collection, it will return a sorted collection. We can nicely configure the Comparator parameter when calling this method.

```
compare/fpij/Compare.java
List<Person> ascendingAge =
  people.stream()
        .sorted((person1, person2) -> person1.ageDifference(person2))
        .collect(toList());
printPeople("Sorted in ascending order by age: ", ascendingAge);
```

We first transformed the given List of people to a Stream using the stream() method. We then invoked the sorted() method on it. This method takes a Comparator as its parameter. Since Comparator is a functional interface, we conveniently passed in a lambda expression. Finally we invoked the collect() method and asked it to put the result into a List. Recall that the collect() method is a reducer that will help to target the members of the transformed iteration into a desirable type or format. The toList() is a static method on the Collectors convenience class.

Comparator's compareTo() abstract method takes two parameters, the objects to be compared, and returns an int result. To comply with this, our lambda expression takes two parameters, two instances of Person, with their types inferred by the Java compiler. We return an int indicating whether the objects are equal.

Since we want to sort by the age property, we compare the two given people's ages and return the difference. If they're the same age, our lambda expression will return a 0 to indicate they're equal. Otherwise, it will indicate the first person is younger by returning a negative number or older by returning a positive number for the age difference.

The sorted() method will iterate over each element in the target collection (people in this example) and apply the given Comparator (a lambda expression in this case) to decide the logical ordering of the elements. The execution mechanism of sorted() is much like the reduce() method we saw earlier. The reduce() method trickles the list down to one value. The sorted() method, on the other hand, uses the result of the comparison to perform the ordering.

Once we sort the instances we want to print the values, so we invoke a convenience method printPeople(); let's write that method next.

compare/fpij/Compare.java

```
public static void printPeople(
  final String message, final List<Person> people) {

  System.out.println(message);
  people.forEach(System.out::println);
}
```

In this method we print a message and iterate over the given collection, printing each of the instances.

Let's call the sorted() method, and the people in the list will be printed in ascending order by age.

```
Sorted in ascending order by age:
John - 20
Sara - 21
Jane - 21
Greg - 35
```

Let's revisit the call to the sorted() method and make one more improvement to it.

```
.sorted((person1, person2) -> person1.ageDifference(person2))
```

In the lambda expression we're passing to the sorted() method, we're simply routing the two parameters—the first parameter as the target to the ageDifference() method and the second as its argument. Rather than writing this code, we can use the office-space pattern—i.e., ask the Java compiler to do the routing again, using a method reference.

The parameter routing we want here is a bit different from the ones we saw earlier. So far we've seen a parameter being used as a target in one case and as an argument in another case. In the current situation, however, we have two parameters and we want those to be split, the first to be used as a target to the method and the second as an argument. No worries. The Java compiler gives us a friendly nod: "I can take care of that for you."

Let's replace the lambda expression in the previous call to the sorted() method with a short and sweet reference to the ageDifference() method.

```
people.stream()
    .sorted(Person::ageDifference)
```

The code is fantastically concise, thanks to the method-reference convenience the Java compiler offers. The compiler took the parameters, the two person instances being compared, and made the first the ageDifference() method's target and the second the parameter. Rather than explicitly connecting these, we let the compiler work a little extra for us. When using this conciseness, we must be careful to ensure that the first parameter is really the intended target of the method referenced and the remaining parameters are its arguments.

Reusing a Comparator

We got the people sorted in ascending order by age quite easily, and sorting them in descending order is just as easy. Let's give that a shot.

```
compare/fpij/Compare.java
printPeople("Sorted in descending order by age: ",
  people.stream()
      .sorted((person1, person2) -> person2.ageDifference(person1))
      .collect(toList()));
```

We called the sorted() method and passed a lambda expression that conforms to the Comparator interface, much like the previous time. The only difference is the implementation of the lambda expression—we switched the people in the age comparison. The result should be a sort by descending order of their ages. Let's look at the output.

```
Sorted in descending order by age:
Greg - 35
Sara - 21
Jane - 21
John - 20
```

Changing the logic for our comparison was effortless. We can't quite refactor this version to use the method reference, though, because the parameter order here does not follow the parameter-routing conventions for method reference; the first parameter is not used as a target to the method, but rather as its argument. There's a way to fix that, and in the process remove a duplication of effort that crept in. Let's see how.

Earlier we created two lambda expressions: one to order the ages of two people in ascending order and the other to do it in descending order. In so doing, we duplicated the logic and the effort, and violated the DRY principle.[1] If all we want is a reverse of the comparison, the JDK has us covered with a reversed() method on the Comparator, marked with a special method modifier called default. We'll discuss default methods in *A Peek into the default Methods*, on page 77, but here we'll use the new reversed() method to remove the duplication.

compare/fpij/Compare.java

```
Comparator<Person> compareAscending =
  (person1, person2) -> person1.ageDifference(person2);
Comparator<Person> compareDescending = compareAscending.reversed();
```

We first created a Comparator, compareAscending, to compare the age of the people in ascending order using the lambda expression syntax. To reverse the order of comparison instead of duplicating the effort, we can simply call reversed() on the first Comparator to get another Comparator with the comparison orders in reverse. Under the hood the reversed() creates a comparator that swaps its parameters' order of comparison. This makes the reversed() method a higher-order method—this function creates and returns another functional expression with no side effect. Let's use these two comparators in the code.

compare/fpij/Compare.java

```
printPeople("Sorted in ascending order by age: ",
  people.stream()
        .sorted(compareAscending)
        .collect(toList())
);
printPeople("Sorted in descending order by age: ",
  people.stream()
        .sorted(compareDescending)
        .collect(toList())
);
```

It's becoming clear how the new features in Java 8 can greatly reduce code complexity and duplication of effort, but to get all the benefits we have to explore the seemingly endless possibilities the JDK offers.

We've been sorting by age, but we could sort by name quite easily, as well. Let's sort in ascending alphabetical order by name; again, only the logic within the lambda expression needs to change.

compare/fpij/Compare.java

```
printPeople("Sorted in ascending order by name: ",
  people.stream()
        .sorted((person1, person2) ->
            person1.getName().compareTo(person2.getName()))
        .collect(toList()));
```

---

1. http://c2.com/cgi/wiki?DontRepeatYourself

In the output we should now see the people with names listed in ascending alphabetical order.

```
Sorted in ascending order by name:
Greg - 35
Jane - 21
John - 20
Sara - 21
```

So far our comparisons have worked on either the age or the name property. We can make the logic in the lambda expression more intelligent. For example, we could sort based on both name and age.

Let's pick the youngest person in the list. We could find the first person after we've sorted by age in ascending order. But we don't need to go that far; the Stream has us covered with a min() method. This method also accepts a Comparator but returns the smallest object in the collection based on the given comparator. Let's use that method.

```
compare/fpij/Compare.java
people.stream()
      .min(Person::ageDifference)
      .ifPresent(youngest -> System.out.println("Youngest: " + youngest));
```

We use the reference for the ageDifference() method in the call to the min() method. The min() method returns an Optional because the list may be empty and therefore there may not be a youngest person. We then print the details of the youngest person that we get access to from the Optional using its ifPresent() method. Let's look at the output.

```
Youngest: John - 20
```

We can as easily find the oldest person in the list. Simply pass that method reference to a max() method.

```
compare/fpij/Compare.java
people.stream()
      .max(Person::ageDifference)
      .ifPresent(eldest -> System.out.println("Eldest: " + eldest));
```

Let's look at the output for the name and age of the oldest in the list.

```
Eldest: Greg - 35
```

We saw how lambda expressions and method references make implementing comparators concise and easy. For its part, the JDK has evolved with a few convenience methods added to the Comparator interface to make comparisons more fluent, as we'll see next.

Multiple and Fluent Comparisons

Let's look at the new convenience methods added to the Comparator interface and use them to compare with ease based on multiple properties.

We'll continue with the example from the previous section. To sort people by their name we used this:

```
people.stream()
    .sorted((person1, person2) ->
      person1.getName().compareTo(person2.getName()));
```

The syntax is quite concise compared to the inner-classes syntax from yesteryear. But we can do better thanks to convenience functions in the Comparator interface. We can more fluently express our objectives using them. For example, to sort people by comparing their names, we can write this:

```
compare/fpij/Compare.java
final Function<Person, String> byName = person -> person.getName();
people.stream()
    .sorted(comparing(byName));
```

In the code we statically imported the comparing() method in the Comparator interface. The comparing() method uses the logic embedded in the provided lambda expression to create a Comparator. In other words, it's a higher-order function that takes in one function (Function) and returns another (Comparator). In addition to making the syntax more concise, the code now reads fluently to express the problem being solved.

We can take this fluency further to make multiple comparisons. For example, here is some cogent syntax to sort people in ascending order by both age and name:

```
compare/fpij/Compare.java
final Function<Person, Integer> byAge = person -> person.getAge();
final Function<Person, String> byTheirName = person -> person.getName();

printPeople("Sorted in ascending order by age and name: ",
  people.stream()
      .sorted(comparing(byAge).thenComparing(byTheirName))
      .collect(toList()));
```

We first created two lambda expressions, one to return the age of a given person and the other to return that person's name. We then combined these two lambda expressions in the call to the sorted() method to compare on both properties. The comparing() method created and returned a Comparator to compare based on age. On the returned Comparator we invoked the thenComparing() method to create a composite comparator that compares based on both age and name. The output from this code shows the net result of sorting by age first and then by name.

```
Sorted in ascending order by age and name:
John - 20
Jane - 21
Sara - 21
Greg - 35
```

As we can see, it's easy to combine the Comparator implementations using the convenience of lambda expressions and the new utility classes in the JDK. Next we'll examine Collectors.

Using the collect Method and the Collectors Class

We've used the collect() method a few times in the examples to gather Stream elements into an ArrayList. This method is a *reduce* operation that's useful for transforming the collection into another form, often a mutable collection. The collect() function, when combined with the utility methods of the Collectors class, provides a wealth of conveniences, as we'll see in this section.

Let's examine the power of collect() using the Person list as an example. Suppose we want to collect only people older than 20 years from the original list. Here's a version that uses mutability and forEach().

```
compare/fpij/OlderThan20.java
List<Person> olderThan20 = new ArrayList<>();
  people.stream()
        .filter(person -> person.getAge() > 20)
        .forEach(person -> olderThan20.add(person));
System.out.println("People older than 20: " + olderThan20);
```

From the Person list we filtered only people who are older than 20 years using the filter() method. Then, within the forEach() method, we added the elements into an ArrayList we initialized before starting the iteration. Let's look at the output from this code before we refactor it.

```
People older than 20: [Sara - 21, Jane - 21, Greg - 35]
```

The code produced the desired result, but there are a few issues. First, the operation of adding an element into the target collection is pretty low level—imperative rather than declarative. If we decide to make the iteration concurrent, we immediately have to deal with thread-safety concerns—the mutability makes it hard to parallelize. Fortunately, we can easily alleviate these concerns using the collect() method. Let's see how.

The collect() method takes a stream of elements and *collects* or gathers them into a result container. To do that, the method needs to know three things:

- How to make a result container (for example, using the ArrayList::new method)

- How to add a single element to a result container (for example, using the ArrayList::add method)

- How to merge one result container into another (for example, using the ArrayList::addAll method)

The last item may not be necessary for purely sequential operations; the code is designed to work for both sequential and parallel execution.

Let's provide these operations to the collect() method to gather the results of a stream after a filter operation.

```
compare/fpij/OlderThan20.java
List<Person> olderThan20 =
  people.stream()
        .filter(person -> person.getAge() > 20)
        .collect(ArrayList::new, ArrayList::add, ArrayList::addAll);
System.out.println("People older than 20: " + olderThan20);
```

This version of code produces the same result as the previous version; however, this version has many benefits.

First, we're programming with intention and more expressively, clearly indicating our goal of collecting the result into an ArrayList. The collect() method took a factory or supplier as the first parameter, followed by operations that help accumulate elements into the collection.

Second, since we're not performing any explicit mutation in code, it's easy to parallelize the execution of the iteration. Since we let the library control the mutation, it can handle coordination and thread safety for us. This is in spite of the fact that ArrayList is not itself thread safe—nifty.

The collect() method can perform parallel additions, as appropriate, into different sublists, and then merge them in a thread-safe manner into a larger list (hence the last parameter to help merge lists).

We saw the benefits of the collect() method over manually adding elements into an ArrayList. Next let's look at another overloaded version of this method that's simpler and more convenient—it uses a Collector as the parameter. The Collector rolls into an interface the operations of supplier, accumulator, and combiner —the operations we specified as three separate parameters in the previous example—for ease and reuse. The Collectors utility class provides a toList()

convenience method that creates an implementation of the Collector interface to accumulate elements into an ArrayList. Let's modify the previous version to use this version of collect.

compare/fpij/OlderThan20.java
```
List<Person> olderThan20 =
  people.stream()
        .filter(person -> person.getAge() > 20)
        .collect(Collectors.toList());
System.out.println("People older than 20: " + olderThan20);
```

The convenience of this concise version of collect() along with the Collectors utility doesn't stop here. There are several methods on the Collectors to perform various collect or accumulate operations. For example, in addition to toList(), there is toSet() to accumulate into a set, toMap() to gather into a key-value collection, and joining() to concatenate the elements into a string. We can also join multiple combine operations using methods like mapping(), collectingAndThen(), minBy(), maxBy(), and groupingBy().

Let's use groupingBy() to group people by their age.

compare/fpij/OlderThan20.java
```
Map<Integer, List<Person>> peopleByAge =
  people.stream()
        .collect(Collectors.groupingBy(Person::getAge));
System.out.println("Grouped by age: " + peopleByAge);
```

With a simple call to the collect() method we are able to perform the grouping. The groupingBy() method takes a lambda expression or a method reference—called the *classifier function*—that returns the value of the property on which we want to do the grouping. Based on what we return from this function, it puts the element in context into that bucket or group. We can see the grouping in this output:

```
Grouped by age: {35=[Greg - 35], 20=[John - 20], 21=[Sara - 21, Jane - 21]}
```

The instances of Person are grouped based on their age.

In the previous example we grouped and collected people by age. A variation of the groupingBy() method can combine multiple criteria. The simple groupingBy collector uses the classifier to organize the stream of elements into buckets. The general groupingBy collector, on the other hand, can apply yet another collector to each bucket. In other words, downstream the values collected into buckets can go through more classification and collection, as we'll see next.

Continuing with the previous example, instead of creating a map of all Person objects by age, let's get only people's names, ordered by age.

```
compare/fpij/OlderThan20.java
Map<Integer, List<String>> nameOfPeopleByAge =
  people.stream()
        .collect(
            groupingBy(Person::getAge, mapping(Person::getName, toList())));
System.out.println("People grouped by age: " + nameOfPeopleByAge);
```

In this version groupingBy() takes two parameters: the first is the age, which is the criteria to group by, and the second is a Collector, which is the result of a call to the mapping() function. These methods are from the Collectors utility class, statically imported for use in this code. The mapping() method takes two details, the property on which to map (name in this case) and the type of the object to collect into, such as list or set. Let's look at the output from this code:

```
People grouped by age: {35=[Greg], 20=[John], 21=[Sara, Jane]}
```

We see that the list of names is grouped by age.

Let's look at one more combination: let's group the names by their first character and then get the oldest person in each group.

```
compare/fpij/OlderThan20.java
Comparator<Person> byAge = Comparator.comparing(Person::getAge);
Map<Character, Optional<Person>> oldestPersonOfEachLetter =
  people.stream()
        .collect(groupingBy(person -> person.getName().charAt(0),
            reducing(BinaryOperator.maxBy(byAge))));
System.out.println("Oldest person of each letter:");
System.out.println(oldestPersonOfEachLetter);
```

We first group the names based on their first letter. For this, we pass a lambda expression as the first parameter to the groupingBy() method. From within this lambda expression we return the first character of the name for grouping purposes. The second parameter in this example, instead of mapping, performs a reduce operation. In each group, it reduces the elements to the oldest person, as decided by the maxBy() method. The syntax is a bit dense due to the combination of operations, but it reads like this: *group by first character of name and reduce to the person with maximum age.* Let's look at the output, which lists the oldest person in each grouping of names that start with a given letter.

```
Oldest person of each letter:
{S=Optional[Sara - 21], G=Optional[Greg - 35], J=Optional[Jane - 21]}
```

We've seen the power of the collect() method and the Collectors. Take a few minutes to examine the Collectors utility class in your integrated development environment or the documentation and get familiar with the facilities it offers. Next we'll use lambda expressions to stand in for some filters.

Listing All Files in a Directory

It's pretty simple to use the File class's list() method to list all filenames in a directory. To get all the files instead of just their names, we can use the listFiles() method. That's easy, but the challenge is how to proceed once we get the list. Rather than the long-winded traditional external iterator, we can use the elegant functional-style facility to iterate through the list. To achieve this, we have to reach out to the JDK's new CloseableStream interface, along with some related higher-order convenience functions.

Here's the code to list the names of all the files in the current directory.

```
compare/fpij/ListFiles.java
Files.list(Paths.get("."))
    .forEach(System.out::println);
```

To list files in a different directory, we can replace "." with the full path of the directory we desire.

We first created a Path instance from the string using the get() method of the Paths convenience class. Then, using the list() method of the Files utility class (in the java.nio.file package) we got a new CloseableStream to iterate over the files in the given path. We then used the internal iterator, forEach(), on it to print the filenames. Let's look at part of the output from this code: listing the files and subdirectories of the current directory.

```
./aSampleFiles.txt
./bin
./fpij
...
```

If we want only the subdirectories in the current directory instead of a listing of all the files, we can use the filter() method:

```
compare/fpij/ListDirs.java
Files.list(Paths.get("."))
    .filter(Files::isDirectory)
    .forEach(System.out::println);
```

The filter() method extracted only the directories from the stream of files. Instead of passing in a lambda expression, we provided a method reference to the Files class's isDirectory() method. Recall that the filter() method expects a Predicate, which returns a boolean result, so this method fits the bill. Finally we used the internal iterator to print the names of the directories. The output from this code will show the subdirectories of the current directory.

```
./bin
./fpij
./output
...
```

That was quite simple and took fewer lines than it would have with old-style Java code. Next let's look at listing only select files that match a pattern.

Listing Select Files in a Directory

Java has long provided a variation of the list() method to cherry-pick filenames. This version of list() takes a FilenameFilter as its parameter. This interface has one method, accept(), that takes two parameters: File dir (representing the directory) and String name (representing a filename). We'd return a true from the accept() method to include the given filename in the list, and false otherwise. Let's explore the options to implement this method.

It's a habitual practice in Java to pass to the list() method an instance of an anonymous inner class that implements the FilenameFilter interface. For example, let's look at how we'd select only the java files in a fpij directory using that approach.

```
compare/fpij/ListSelectFiles.java
    final String[] files =
      new File("fpij").list(new java.io.FilenameFilter() {
        public boolean accept(final File dir, final String name) {
          return name.endsWith(".java");
        }
      });
System.out.println(files);
```

That took some effort and a few lines of code. There's a lot of noise in that code: an object creation, a function call, an anonymous inner class definition, the embedded method within that class, and so on. We don't have to endure that pain anymore; we can simply pass a lambda expression that takes two parameters and returns a boolean result. The Java compiler can take care of the rest for us.

While we could simply replace the anonymous inner class with a lambda expression in the previous example, we can do better than that. The new DirectoryStream facility can help traverse large directory structures more efficiently, so let's explore that route. There's a variation of the newDirectoryStream() method, which takes an additional filter parameter.

Let's use lambda expressions to get a list of all java files in the fpij directory.

```
compare/fpij/ListSelectFiles.java
Files.newDirectoryStream(
         Paths.get("fpij"), path -> path.toString().endsWith(".java"))
    .forEach(System.out::println);
```

We got rid of the anonymous inner class and turned the verbose code into short and sweet code. The net effect of the two versions is the same. Let's print the selected files.

The code will display only the .java files in the mentioned directory, as in this partial output:

```
fpij/Compare.java
fpij/IterateString.java
fpij/ListDirs.java
...
```

We picked files based on filenames, but we can easily pick files based on file properties, such as if a file is executable, readable, or writable. For this we need a variation of the listFiles() method that takes FileFilter as its parameter. Once again, we can use lambda expressions instead of creating an anonymous inner class. Let's look at an example of listing all hidden files in the current directory.

```
compare/fpij/ListHiddenFiles.java
final File[] files = new File(".").listFiles(file -> file.isHidden());
```

If we're working with a large directory, then we can use the DirectoryStream instead of directly using the methods on File.

The signature of the lambda expression we passed to the listFiles() method conforms to the signature of the FileFilter interface's accept() method. In the lambda expression we receive a File instance as the parameter, named file in this example. We return a boolean true if the file has the hidden property, and false otherwise.

We can further reduce the code here; rather than passing a lambda expression, we can use a method reference to make the code more concise:

```
compare/fpij/ListHiddenFiles.java
new File(".").listFiles(File::isHidden);
```

We created the lambda-expressions version and then refactored it to the more concise method-references version. When working on new code, it's perfectly OK to take that route. If we can see the concise code from miles away, then of course we can readily key that in. In the spirit of "make it work, then make it better," it's good to get something simple working first, and once we understand the code, we can take the next step to refactor for conciseness, performance, and so on.

We worked through an example to filter out select files from a directory. Next we'll look at how to explore subdirectories of a given directory.

Listing Immediate Subdirectories Using flatMap

We saw how to list the members of a given directory. Let's look at the effort to explore the immediate (one level deep) subdirectories in a given directory, first using a rudimentary operation and then, more conveniently, using the flatMap() method.

Let's use the traditional for loop first to iterate over the files in a given directory. If a subdirectory contains any files, we'll add them to our list; otherwise, we'll add the subdirectory itself to the list. Finally, we'll print the total number of files found. Here's the code—for the hard way.

```
compare/fpij/ListSubDirs.java
public static void listTheHardWay() {
  List<File> files = new ArrayList<>();

  File[] filesInCurrentDir = new File(".").listFiles();
  for(File file : filesInCurrentDir) {
    File[] filesInSubDir = file.listFiles();
    if(filesInSubDir != null) {
      files.addAll(Arrays.asList(filesInSubDir));
    } else {
      files.add(file);
    }
  }

  System.out.println("Count: " + files.size());
}
```

We fetch the list of files in the current directory and loop through each of the files. For each file, we query for its children and add them, if present, to the list of files. That works, but it comes with the usual culprits: mutability, primitive obsession, imperative, noise.... We can get rid of these using a nice little method called flatMap().

As the name indicates, this method will flatten after mapping. It maps the elements in a collection, much like the map() method does. But unlike the map() method, where we generally return an element from the lambda expression, we return a Stream instead. The method then flattens the multiple streams, obtained by mapping each element, into one flat stream.

We can use flatMap() for various operations, but the problem on hand nicely demonstrates the usefulness of this method. Each subdirectory has a list or stream of files and we're trying to get a combined (or flattened) list of files in all the subdirectories of the current directory.

Some directories (or files) may be empty and may not have children. In that case, we simply wrap a stream around the no-child directory or file element. In case we choose to ignore a file, the flatMap() method in the JDK can deal with *empty* quite well; it will merge a null reference to a Stream as an empty collection. Let's see the flatMap() method in action.

```
compare/fpij/ListSubDirs.java
public static void betterWay() {
  List<File> files =
    Stream.of(new File(".").listFiles())
          .flatMap(file -> file.listFiles() == null ?
              Stream.of(file) : Stream.of(file.listFiles()))
          .collect(toList());
  System.out.println("Count: " + files.size());
}
```

We obtained a stream of files in the current directory and invoked the flatMap() method on it. To this method we passed a lambda expression that returns a Stream of children for the given file. The flatMap() returns a flattened map of a collection of all the children of the current directory's subdirectories. We collect those back into a List using the toList() methods of the collect() and Collectors.

The lambda expression we passed as a parameter to the flatMap() method returned, for a given file, a Stream of its children (if any). Otherwise, it returned a stream with just the file. The flatMap() method gracefully handled that and mapped these streams into a resulting collection of streams and finally flattened it into one final Stream of Files.

flatMap() eliminates so much effort—it nicely combines a sequence of two operations, often called as a *monadic composition*—into one single elegant step.

We saw how the flatMap() method simplifies the task of listing the immediate (one level deep) contents of a subdirectory. Next we'll create an observer for file changes.

Watching a File Change

We know how to look for files and directories, but if we want to sit back and get alerts when a file is created, modified, or deleted, that's quite easy as well. Such a facility is useful for monitoring changes to special files like configuration files and system resources. Here we'll explore the facility that's been available since Java 7, the WatchService, to watch for file changes. Most of the features we'll see here are from JDK 7 and the main improvement will be in the convenience of the internal iterator.

Let's create an example to watch for file changes in the current directory. The Path class in the JDK can lead to an instance of the file system, which acts as a factory for the watch service. We can register with this service for any notification, like so:

```
compare/fpij/WatchFileChange.java
final Path path = Paths.get(".");
final WatchService watchService =
  path.getFileSystem()
      .newWatchService();

path.register(watchService, StandardWatchEventKinds.ENTRY_MODIFY);

System.out.println("Report any file changed within next 1 minute...");
```

We've registered a WatchService to observe any change to the current directory. We can *poll* the watch service for any change to files in this directory, and it will notify us through a WatchKey. Once we gain access to the key, we can iterate though all the events to get the details of the file update. Since multiple files may change at once, a poll may return a collection of events rather than a single event. Let's look at the code for polling and iterating.

```
compare/fpij/WatchFileChange.java
final WatchKey watchKey = watchService.poll(1, TimeUnit.MINUTES);

if(watchKey != null) {
  watchKey.pollEvents()
          .stream()
          .forEach(event ->
            System.out.println(event.context()));
}
```

We see an interplay of Java 7 and Java 8 features here. We transformed the collection returned by pollEvents() into a Java 8 Stream and then used an internal iterator on it to display the details of the updated file(s).

Let's run the code, change the sample.txt file in the current directory, and see if the program tattletales about the change.

```
Report any file changed within next 1 minute...
sample.txt
```

When we modified the file, the program promptly reported that the file was changed. We can use this facility to watch for changes to various files and perform appropriate tasks in our applications. Or we could register for only file creation or deletion, as we desire.

Recap

The regular tasks of working with strings and files and creating custom comparators got a lot easier and more concise with lambda expressions and method references. Anonymous inner classes morphed into an elegant style and, along the way, mutability disappeared like the fog in the morning sun. As a bonus for favoring this style, we can benefit from the new JDK facilities to iterate efficiently over large directories.

Now you know how to create lambda expressions to pass as parameters to methods. In the next chapter we'll look at ways to design programs with functional interfaces and lambda expressions.

Design is not just what it looks like and feels like. Design is how it works.

> ➤ *Steve Jobs*

CHAPTER 4

Designing with Lambda Expressions

OOP has become the de facto standard, but with lambda expressions in Java, we can pull a few more techniques out of our bag of design tricks. In Java, OOP and functional style can now complement each other and can nicely interplay. We can use these to create lightweight designs that are flexible to change and easier to extend.

We can replace interfaces, class hierarchies, and anonymous inner classes with concise code. We need fewer lines of code to get the same job done, and we can quickly try out new ideas.

In this chapter lambda expressions bring to life some neat design ideas; where we often use objects, we'll instead use lightweight functions. We'll use lambda expressions to easily separate logic from functions, making them more extensible. Then we'll apply them to delegate responsibilities and implement the decorator pattern in just a couple of lines of code. Finally we'll use them to turn mundane interfaces into fluent, intuitive interfaces.

Separating Concerns Using Lambda Expressions

We often create classes to reuse code; we have good intentions, but it's not always the right choice. By using higher-order functions, we can accomplish the same goals without needing a hierarchy of classes.

Exploring Design Concerns

Let's start with an example to sum asset values as a way to illustrate the design idea of separation of concerns. We'll build it in iterations. The design we first create will mix multiple concerns in one method, but we'll quickly refactor to make the method more cohesive. Let's start with an Asset class.

designing/fpij/Asset.java

```
public class Asset {
  public enum AssetType { BOND, STOCK };
  private final AssetType type;
  private final int value;
  public Asset(final AssetType assetType, final int assetValue) {
    type = assetType;
    value = assetValue;
  }
  public AssetType getType() { return type; }
  public int getValue() { return value; }
}
```

Asset is a simple JavaBean with two properties: type and value. Suppose we're asked to total the values of all the assets given—let's write a method for that in a AssetUtil class.

designing/fpij/AssetUtil.java

```
public static int totalAssetValues(final List<Asset> assets) {
  return assets.stream()
               .mapToInt(Asset::getValue)
               .sum();
}
```

We used the convenience of lambda expressions within this function. We transformed the List of Assets into a Stream, then mapped that into a Stream of values using the mapToInt() method. Finally we reduced or totaled the values in this stream to arrive at a single value using the sum() method. Let's define some assets to try out the code.

designing/fpij/AssetUtil.java

```
final List<Asset> assets = Arrays.asList(
  new Asset(Asset.AssetType.BOND, 1000),
  new Asset(Asset.AssetType.BOND, 2000),
  new Asset(Asset.AssetType.STOCK, 3000),
  new Asset(Asset.AssetType.STOCK, 4000)
);
```

Here's a call to the totalAssetValues() method using these assets.

designing/fpij/AssetUtil.java

```
System.out.println("Total of all assets: " + totalAssetValues(assets));
```

The code will report the total of all the given assets, as we see in the output.

```
Total of all assets: 10000
```

It's good we employed lambda expressions to write the totalAssetValues() method —we used fluent iterators and favored immutability. But let's shift our attention to the design of the method itself. It's tangled with three concerns:

how to iterate, what to total, and how to total. This entangled logic will result in poor reuse. Let's see how.

Getting Entangled with the Concerns

Imagine we're asked to total only the bond assets. After a quick glance at the totalAssetValues() method, we realize it does almost everything we need. Why not copy and paste that code? After all, there's a reason the integrated development environments have gone through the trouble to provide keyboard shortcuts for that, right?

We'll leave totalAssetValues() intact, but duplicate it and modify the new version, like so:

designing/fpij/AssetUtil.java

```
public static int totalBondValues(final List<Asset> assets) {
  return assets.stream()
              .mapToInt(asset ->
                 asset.getType() == AssetType.BOND ? asset.getValue() : 0)
              .sum();
}
```

The only difference, other than their names, between totalBondValues() and totalAssetValues() is in the lambda expressions we send to the mapToInt() function. In this newer method we pick the price of the asset if it's a bond; otherwise we use a 0 for the price. Instead of crowding the logic within that one lambda expression we could use a filter() method to extract only bonds, and leave the lambda expression that was passed to the mapToInt() method untouched from the version copied from the totalAssetValues() method.

Let's call this version of the method and make sure it works.

designing/fpij/AssetUtil.java

```
System.out.println("Total of bonds: " + totalBondValues(assets));
```

The output should report only the total of bond prices.

```
Total of bonds: 3000
```

As fate may have it, now we're asked to total only stocks. We know it's morally wrong to copy and paste code once more, but no one's looking.

designing/fpij/AssetUtil.java

```
public static int totalStockValues(final List<Asset> assets) {
  return assets.stream()
              .mapToInt(asset ->
                 asset.getType() == AssetType.STOCK ? asset.getValue() : 0)
              .sum();
}
```

Let's call this version of the method too:

designing/fpij/AssetUtil.java
```
System.out.println("Total of stocks: " + totalStockValues(assets));
```

The output gives us the desired results: a total of stocks only.

```
Total of stocks: 7000
```

Hey, it works and we even used lambda expressions. Time to call it done and celebrate?

Not quite; if our geeky friends discover the duplicates, they'll no longer hang out with us. We need a better design: one that's DRY,[1] one that'll make mothers proud.

Refactoring to Separate a Key Concern

Let's revisit the three methods. They share two out of the three concerns we mentioned earlier. The iteration and the way to total are the same. The "what to total" concern is different and is a good candidate to separate out of these methods.

This seems like a good place for the *strategy* pattern (see Gamma et al.'s *Design Patterns: Elements of Reusable Object-Oriented Software [GHJV95]*). We often create interfaces and classes to implement that pattern in Java, but here lambda expressions will give us a design edge.

Let's refactor the three methods into one that takes a functional interface as a parameter.

designing/fpij/AssetUtilRefactored.java
```
public static int totalAssetValues(final List<Asset> assets,
  final Predicate<Asset> assetSelector) {
  return assets.stream()
              .filter(assetSelector)
              .mapToInt(Asset::getValue)
              .sum();
}
```

This refactored version of totalAssetValues() takes two parameters: the list of assets and a Predicate to evaluate whether an asset should be considered.

At first this may look like what we would've done all along in Java, but it's different in a few ways. Rather than creating our own interface, we've reused the java.util.function.Predicate interface from the JDK. Furthermore, instead of

---

1.   http://c2.com/cgi/wiki?DontRepeatYourself

creating classes or anonymous inner classes, we can pass lambda expressions to the refactored version of the totalAssetValue() method.

Let's dig into this refactored version. We filtered the list of assets using the filter() method, then mapped the assets to their prices using the mapToInt() function, and totaled them. We simply passed the Predicate we received on to the filter() method and used a method reference for the mapToInt()'s argument.

The filter method takes care of picking only the assets we're interested in. Under the hood, it calls the given Predicate's test() method to make that decision. If the selector accepted the asset, we use its value to total further down in the chain.

With this refactoring, we turned the three normal methods into one higher-order function that depends on a lightweight strategy to handle a configurable concern, as the next figure illustrates.

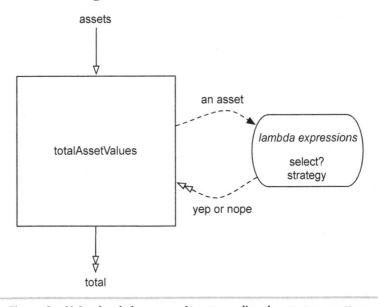

Figure 3—Using lambda expressions to realize the strategy pattern

Let's use this refactored version of totalAssetValues() to total the values of all the assets.

```
designing/fpij/AssetUtilRefactored.java
System.out.println("Total of all assets: " +
  totalAssetValues(assets, asset -> true));
```

We invoke the totalAssetValues() function, passing it the list of assets as the first argument and a succinct lambda expression as the second argument. As the function iterates over the assets, it invokes the lambda expression for each asset, asking if the asset's value should be included in the total. Since we want to total all the assets, we return a boolean true here.

We've used the *open/closed principle* in this refactored design.[2] We can easily change the selection criteria without changing the method, as we'll see next.

Let's reuse the function to compute the total of only bonds and then the total of only stocks. We'll pass different lambda expressions as the second argument to the totalAssetValues() function.

```
designing/fpij/AssetUtilRefactored.java
System.out.println("Total of bonds: " +
  totalAssetValues(assets, asset -> asset.getType() == AssetType.BOND));

System.out.println("Total of stocks: " +
  totalAssetValues(assets, asset -> asset.getType() == AssetType.STOCK));
```

Let quickly run these last three calls to the refactored totalAssetValues() function to ensure the output is the same as that of the previous version.

```
Total of all assets: 10000
Total of bonds: 3000
Total of stocks: 7000
```

We've used lambda expressions to separate the concern from the method. This is a simple use of the strategy pattern, but without the burden of creating extra classes. This pattern does require a bit more from the higher-order function's users—they have to chose the selection logic. However, they can save these lambda expressions into variables and reuse them if they desire.

We focused on concerns at a method level in this section; let's apply that technique at the class level next.

Delegating Using Lambda Expressions

We used lambda expressions and the strategy pattern to separate a concern from a method. We can also use them to separate a concern from a class. From a reuse point of view, delegation is a better design tool than inheritance. With delegation it's easier to vary the implementation we rely on, and we can plug in a different behavior more dynamically. This can help vary the behavior of classes independent of the behavior of the parts they depend on, and make the design more flexible without forcing a deep class hierarchy.

---

2.   http://en.wikipedia.org/wiki/Open/closed_principle

Creating a Delegate

Rather than delegating part of the responsibility to another class, we can delegate it to lambda expressions and method references. This will further reduce class proliferation. Let's explore that idea with an example; we'll start with a class, CalculateNAV, that performs financial calculations with data from a web service.

```
designing/fpij/CalculateNAV.java
public class CalculateNAV {
  public BigDecimal computeStockWorth(
    final String ticker, final int shares) {
    return priceFinder.apply(ticker).multiply(BigDecimal.valueOf(shares));
  }
  //... other methods that use the priceFinder ...
}
```

In the computeStockWorth() method we request the price of a ticker from a (yet to be defined) priceFinder and determine the net worth based on the number of shares. The CalculateNAV may have other methods to perform other calculations, such as yield, with the price returned by the priceFinder. That's a reason for the priceFinder to be a field in the class rather than a parameter to one particular method of CalculateNAV.

Now we need the priceFinder; we have to decide what kind of object it will be. We want to send in a ticker symbol and receive a price, hopefully obtained from a web service. The java.util.function.Function<T, R> functional interface seems like a good lightweight fit for our needs. Its abstract method can take in a value and return another value, of possibly a different type. Let's use that to define the field.

```
designing/fpij/CalculateNAV.java
private Function<String, BigDecimal> priceFinder;
```

In the computeStockWorth() method we're already using the Function interface's apply() method. Let's initialize the field through a constructor injection rather than coupling to an implementation directly within the class. In effect we're using dependency injection and the *dependency inversion principle*.[3] Instead of embedding an implementation, we'll separate the concern and rely on an abstraction. This will make the code more extensible and help shorten the coding and testing time. Here's the constructor for the CalculateNAV class.

```
designing/fpij/CalculateNAV.java
public CalculateNAV(final Function<String, BigDecimal> aPriceFinder) {
  priceFinder = aPriceFinder;
}
```

---

3. http://c2.com/cgi/wiki?DependencyInversionPrinciple

We're all set to use CalculateNAV, but we need to implement a call to the web service. Let's look into that next.

Stubbing the Web Service

We're focused on the design of CalculateNAV; we want to quickly run it and get feedback. When test-driving the design of this class using unit tests, we don't want to depend on external services—that would make the tests brittle. We want to stub the web service.

In general, though, creating a stub (or mock) in Java can be arduous and we often rely on libraries. Thanks to the lambda expressions and their fluency, this just got easier. Let's create a unit test to try out our computeStockWorth() method, stubbing away the implementation of the apply() method.

designing/fpij/CalculateNAVTest.java
```java
public class CalculateNAVTest {
  @Test
  public void computeStockWorth() {
    final CalculateNAV calculateNAV =
      new CalculateNAV(ticker -> new BigDecimal("6.01"));
    BigDecimal expected = new BigDecimal("6010.00");
    assertEquals(0,
      calculateNAV.computeStockWorth("GOOG", 1000).compareTo(expected),
      0.001);
  }
  //...
}
```

Creating the test was effortless. We passed a lambda expression to the CalculateNAV constructor—this is lightweight stubbing of the web service. From within the lambda expression, we returned a contrived value for the price in response to the call. Then, in the test, we asserted that the computeStockWorth() returned the expected result, within a tolerance of 0.001, for a given ticker and the number of shares.

We can also assert that the ticker passed to the lambda expression is the right one. We can take this further quite easily to add other tests—for example, an exception test to ensure code properly handles web-service failures. We can do all this without really spending time to create the code to talk to the web service, but instead merely stubbing away the implementation. Let's run the test and ensure JUnit reports it passing.

```
.
Time: ...

OK (1 test)
```

Testing the code was quick; we easily stubbed away the dependency to the web service, which helped to rapidly develop and test the code. But we can't call it done until we run it with a real web service. That's our next task.

Integrating with the Web Service

Talking to the real web service is almost as easy—let's invite Yahoo! to the party.

designing/fpij/CalculateNAV.java
```
final CalculateNAV calculateNav = new CalculateNAV(YahooFinance::getPrice);

System.out.println(String.format("100 shares of Google worth: $%.2f",
  calculateNav.computeStockWorth("GOOG", 100)));
```

Rather than stubbing away the implementation here, we pass a method reference to YahooFinance's getPrice() method. We need to implement that method to complete this task.

designing/fpij/YahooFinance.java
```
public class YahooFinance {
  public static BigDecimal getPrice(final String ticker) {
    try {
      final URL url =
        new URL("http://ichart.finance.yahoo.com/table.csv?s=" + ticker);

      final BufferedReader reader =
        new BufferedReader(new InputStreamReader(url.openStream()));
      final String data = reader.lines().skip(1).findFirst().get();
      final String[] dataItems = data.split(",");
      return new BigDecimal(dataItems[dataItems.length - 1]);
    } catch(Exception ex) {
      throw new RuntimeException(ex);
    }
  }
}
```

In the getPrice() method we send a request to the Yahoo! web service and parse the response to extract the stock price. The data we're looking for is in the second line of the multiline response from Yahoo!. Instead of reading line by line from the BufferedReader, we use the new lines() method, an internal iterator that returns a Stream. From this we extract the second line and the data we desire. Let's now exercise the call to the computeStockWorth() method we wrote.

```
100 shares of Google worth: $104593.00
```

In the output we see the worth of 100 shares of Google stock at the time the code was executed. If we run the code now, the value may be something insanely higher—let's hope.

We have to figure out a way to deal with exceptions that may arise when calling the web service. Suppressing exceptions with empty catch blocks or printing them in arbitrary places is pure evil. Rather than dealing with exceptions within lambda expressions, we have to find the right place to handle them. That requires us to rethrow the exceptions so they can be handled upstream.

Lambda expressions and method references can throw checked exceptions only if those exceptions are declared using the throws clause in the abstract method of the functional interface they stand in for. Since the Function interface's apply() method doesn't specify any expected exceptions, we can't directly throw the checked exception in this example. As a workaround, we wrapped the exception into the unchecked RuntimeException. The lambda expression now simply passes the exception through, and upstream in the code we'll have to handle it. Any runtime exception that is not handled, of course, will abruptly terminate the application.

We delegated part of the responsibility of our class using lambda expressions and method references in this example, as the next figure demonstrates.

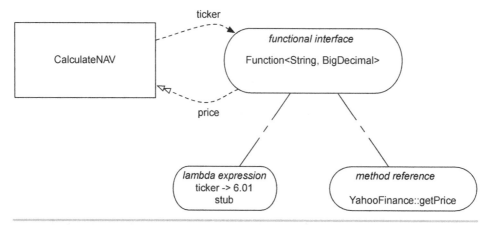

Figure 4—The **CalculateNAV** class delegating the task of getting a stock price

The approach we took helped vary the implementation of the call to the web service and stub it away. Next we'll use lambda expressions to combine multiple behaviors.

Decorating Using Lambda Expressions

So far we've avoided creating implementation classes to support the delegate interfaces. We needed simple implementations for these interfaces, so that worked out fairly well. Let's increase our demands on these implementations, ask them to interact with multiple delegates, and see how lambda expressions handle that.

Delegation is great, but we can take it further if we can chain delegates to add behavior. We can then create discrete flavors of behavior and sprinkle them onto the classes, like the mix-ins at the ice-cream shop.

The decorator pattern is powerful, but programmers often hesitate to use it due to the burdensome hierarchy of classes and interfaces—like FilterInputStream and FilterOutputStream in the JDK—that are used to implement the pattern (see Gamma et al.'s *Design Patterns: Elements of Reusable Object-Oriented Software [GHJV95]*). We can now realize this pattern with less effort in Java.

In the next example we'll chain delegates—using lambda expressions, of course—to realize the decorator pattern. This will help us see how we can create flexible and extensible lightweight design with just a few lines of code.

Designing Filters

Adding filters to a camera is a good example of chaining behavior or responsibilities. We may start with no filters, then add a filter, and then a few more. We want our design to be flexible so that it does not care how many filters we have. Let's create an example Camera that'll use filters to process the captured colors.

```
designing/fpij/Camera.java
@SuppressWarnings("unchecked")
public class Camera {
  private Function<Color, Color> filter;

  public Color capture(final Color inputColor) {
    final Color processedColor = filter.apply(inputColor);
    //... more processing of color...
    return processedColor;
  }

  //... other functions that use the filter ...
}
```

The Camera has a field for the filter, a reference to an instance of Function (much like the delegation example we saw earlier). This filter function can receive a Color and return a processed Color. Looking at what we have so far, the class may appear to use only one filter, but with a design tweak we'll make it work with multiple filters.

To achieve this flexibility, we'll use a method that belongs to a special type called default methods, which is new to Java 8. In addition to abstract methods, interfaces can have methods with implementation, marked as default. These methods are automatically added to the classes that implement the interfaces. This was done as a trick in Java 8 to enhance existing classes with new methods without having to change each one of them. In addition, interfaces can have static methods.

In addition to the apply() abstract method, the Function interface has a default method, compose(), to combine or chain multiple Functions. Within the lambda expression that stands in for a Function parameter, we can readily use this method.

The compose() method can combine or chain two Functions together. Once we compose them, a call to apply() will hop through the chained Functions. Let's take a quick look at how that works. Suppose we compose two Functions, target and next, like this:

```
wrapper = target.compose(next);
```

Now let's invoke the apply() method on the resulting wrapper.

```
wrapper.apply(input);
```

The result of that call is the same as doing this:

```
temp = target.apply(input);
return next.apply(temp);
```

Without the temporary variable, it would be like this:

```
return next.apply(target.apply(input));
```

Let's write a setFilters() method that takes a *varargs* of Function; we can send zero or more filters to this function. In addition, let's create the constructor for the Camera.

```
designing/fpij/Camera.java
public void setFilters(final Function<Color, Color>... filters) {
  filter =
    Stream.of(filters)
          .reduce((filter, next) -> filter.compose(next))
          .orElse(color -> color);
}
public Camera() { setFilters(); }
```

In the setFilters() method we iterate through the filters and compose them into a chain using the compose() method. If no filter is given, then the reduce() method (we saw this method in *Reducing a Collection to a Single Value*, on page 35) will return an Optional empty. In that case we provide a dummy filter as an argument to the orElse() method, and it simply returns the color that the filter would receive for processing. If we provide filters to the setFilters() method, the filter field will refer to the first filter—an instance of Function<Color, Color>—that's at the head of a chain of filters.

We provided a lambda expression as a parameter to the orElse() method of the Optional that the reduce() method returned. The Function interface has an identity() static method that does the same operation as the lambda expression we wrote. Instead of creating our own lambda expression, we can use a reference to that method instead. To do so, we need to change

```
.orElse(color -> color);
```

to

```
.orElseGet(Function::identity);
```

In addition to the setFilters() method we have a constructor that simply sets the filter to the dummy filter I mentioned previously.

Our design of the camera with filters is complete, so let's try it out. We'll use it with no filters first, but we need a Camera instance to start. Let's create one and assign it to a local variable camera.

designing/fpij/Camera.java
```
final Camera camera = new Camera();
final Consumer<String> printCaptured = (filterInfo) ->
  System.out.println(String.format("with %s: %s", filterInfo,
    camera.capture(new Color(200, 100, 200))));
```

To see the camera in action, we need a convenience function to print the capture() method's results. Rather than creating a standalone static method, we created a lambda expression to stand in for an instance of the Consumer functional interface, right here within the main() method. We chose a Consumer because printing consumes the value and does not yield any results. This function will invoke capture() with the colors 200, 100, 200 for the *red*, *green*, and *blue* parts of color, respectively, and print the resulting filtered/processed output. Let's ask the camera to capture the given colors.

designing/fpij/Camera.java
```
printCaptured.accept("no filter");
```

Since no filters are given, the captured color should be the same as the input; let's verify that in the output.

```
with no filter: java.awt.Color[r=200,g=100,b=200]
```

Adding a Filter

Adding a filter is a breeze; we simply have to pass the filter to the setFilters() method. The filter can be a simple lambda expression or a method reference. We can use brighter() on the java.awt.Color class as a filter, so let's simply pass a reference of this method to the setFilters() method.

designing/fpij/Camera.java
```
camera.setFilters(Color::brighter);
printCaptured.accept("brighter filter");
```

Let's look at the result of the capture() with this filter in place.

```
with brighter filter: java.awt.Color[r=255,g=142,b=255]
```

The input color has been brightened. As we can see, the output RGB values are higher than the corresponding values in the input. Let's quickly change the filter to a darker shade.

designing/fpij/Camera.java
```
camera.setFilters(Color::darker);
printCaptured.accept("darker filter");
```

This should reduce the brightness of the input, as we can see in the output.

```
with darker filter: java.awt.Color[r=140,g=70,b=140]
```

Adding Multiple Filters

The design is good so far; now let's mix two filters—a brighter one and a darker one—to see the effect of chaining.

designing/fpij/Camera.java
```
camera.setFilters(Color::brighter, Color::darker);
printCaptured.accept("brighter & darker filter");
```

We passed two method references to the setFilters() method—just essence, no ceremony. (We could've passed in lambda expressions instead of method references.) The two filters are now chained and the filter reference in the Camera instance is referring to the head of the chain. A call to the capture() method will now route the color processing through each of these filters, as we see in Figure 5, *Implementation of the decorator pattern or chaining using lambda expressions*, on page 77.

With this filter combination, the input color goes through a series of transformations or filtering; first it passes through the bright filter, which brightens the shades, then it goes through the dark filter, which makes the colors darker again, as we can see from the output.

```
with brighter & darker filter: java.awt.Color[r=200,g=100,b=200]
```

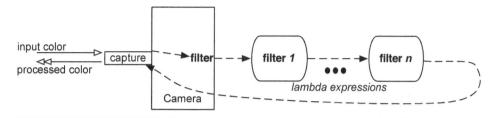

Figure 5—Implementation of the decorator pattern or chaining using lambda expressions

Adding more than two filters is no different; we simply pass more comma-separated filters, either as method references or as lambda expressions.

We designed object chaining and implemented the decorator pattern without having to create a hierarchy of classes. The magic happens in just a couple of lines of code within the setFilters() method. We made good use of the JDK Function interface here. We saw lambda expressions and method references really shine in this example.

We ran into another new Java 8 feature in this section: the default methods. Let's take a closer look at them next.

A Peek into the default Methods

In the design we explored in the previous section we used the new default methods. default methods are not intrinsically tied to lambda expressions or the functional style of programming. However, many of the convenience methods in collections would not have been possible without them.

Interface evolution is the key motivation behind default methods. The API defined in the early '90s was a good idea back then, but for the platform to stay relevant it needs to evolve. The default methods provide a nondisruptive path for that. Moving forward, when we design with interfaces we'll likely use default methods. Let's examine their behavior and how they intermix with classes.

The Java compiler follows a few simple rules to resolve default methods:

1. Subtypes automatically carry over the default methods from their supertypes.

2. For interfaces that contribute a default method, the implementation in a subtype takes precedence over the one in supertypes.

3. Implementations in classes, including abstract declarations, take precedence over all interface defaults.

4. If there's a conflict between two or more default method implementations, or there's a default-abstract conflict between two interfaces, the inheriting class should disambiguate.

To get a better understanding of these rules, let's create an example with default methods.

```java
public interface Fly {
  default void takeOff() { System.out.println("Fly::takeOff"); }
  default void land() { System.out.println("Fly::land"); }
  default void turn() { System.out.println("Fly::turn"); }
  default void cruise() { System.out.println("Fly::cruise"); }
}

public interface FastFly extends Fly {
  default void takeOff() { System.out.println("FastFly::takeOff"); }
}

public interface Sail {
  default void cruise() { System.out.println("Sail::cruise"); }
  default void turn() { System.out.println("Sail::turn"); }
}

public class Vehicle {
  public void turn() { System.out.println("Vehicle::turn"); }
}
```

All the interfaces in this example have default methods. The FastFly interface extends from the Fly interface and overrides the takeOff() method, providing its own default implementation. FastFly also carries forward the other three methods of the Fly interface (*rule 1*). Any class or interface inheriting from FastFly will see the implementation of takeOff() in FastFly, and not the implementation in Fly (*rule 2*).

All three interfaces have implementations for the cruise() and turn() methods. In addition, the Vehicle class implements the turn() method.

Let's create a class that inherits these types.

```java
public class SeaPlane extends Vehicle implements FastFly, Sail {
  private int altitude;
  //...
  public void cruise() {
    System.out.print("SeaPlane::cruise currently cruise like: ");
    if(altitude > 0)
      FastFly.super.cruise();
    else
      Sail.super.cruise();
  }
}
```

SeaPlane extends Vehicle and implements the FastFly and Sail interfaces. Let's take a closer look at the implementation of this class.

There appears to be a conflict for the turn() method, but that's really not the case. Even though the turn() method is present in the interfaces, the implementation in the superclass Vehicle takes precedence here (*rule 3*), so there's no conflict to resolve.

However, the Java compiler will force us to implement the cruise() method in the SeaPlane class because the default implementations in the interfaces FastFly (derived from Fly) and Sail conflict (*rule 4*).

From within the overridden methods we can call back into the corresponding default methods. For example, from within the cruise() method, we can see how to call the default methods of both the FastFly and the Sail interfaces.

We can see the logic of why we'd need to specify the interface name, like FastFly or Sail, when invoking the default methods from within the overriding method. At first glance the use of super may appear superfluous, but it's required. That's how the Java compiler knows if we're referring to a default method (when super is used) or a static method in the interface. In Java 8, interfaces can optionally have default methods and static methods, possibly with the same name.

To see the behavior of the default methods in action, let's create an instance of SeaPlane and invoke the methods on it.

```
SeaPlane seaPlane = new SeaPlane();
seaPlane.takeOff();
seaPlane.turn();
seaPlane.cruise();
seaPlane.land();
```

Before running the code on the computer, we'll run it mentally; let's go over the code to ensure we've understood the rules.

The call to the takeOff() method should go to the implementation in the FastFly interface (*rules 1 and 2*). The implementation of the turn() method in Vehicle should be picked for the call to the turn() method on the SeaPlane, even though these are available on the interfaces (*rule 3*). Since we were forced to implement the cruise() method on the SeaPlane, that specific implementation of the method should be invoked for the call to cruise() (*rule 4*). Finally, the call to the land() method will land on the implementation in the Fly interface (*rule 1*).

We can now compare the output we got from the mental run of the code with the output from the run on the computer:

```
FastFly::takeOff
Vehicle::turn
SeaPlane::cruise currently cruise like: Sail::cruise
Fly::land
```

We used default methods in interfaces, whereas in the past interfaces were allowed to have only abstract methods. Seeing this, it may seem that interfaces have evolved into abstract classes, but that's not the case. Abstract classes can have state, but interfaces can't—this eliminates the concerns of the "diamond problem" of collision from multiple inheritance. Also, we can inherit (implement) a class from multiple interfaces, but we only inherit (extend) from at most one abstract class. The good old recommendation to favor interfaces over abstract classes where possible is still a nice rule to follow. And now, thanks to the ability to have default methods, interfaces are even more attractive and powerful than before.

Now that we understand the behavior of default methods, let's shift our attention back to lambda expressions. So far in this chapter, we've seen the different forms the lambda expressions can take and the multiple design goals we were able to achieve using them. Next we'll cover how they can influence a class's interface.

Creating Fluent Interfaces Using Lambda Expressions

We've been looking at the internals of methods and classes in this chapter. Now let's shift our focus to see how lambda expressions can help shape a class's skin or interface. We can use these techniques to structure the API of our classes, to make it more intuitive and fluent for programmers to use.

Starting with a Design

Let's start with a simple Mailer class and evolve the design of its interface.

designing/fpij/Mailer.java
```java
public class Mailer {
  public void from(final String address) { /*... */ }
  public void to(final String address)   { /*... */ }
  public void subject(final String line) { /*... */ }
  public void body(final String message) { /*... */ }
  public void send() { System.out.println("sending..."); }

  //...
}
```

The class looks routine—a bunch of void methods. Let's use this class to configure and send out an email.

```
designing/fpij/Mailer.java
Mailer mailer = new Mailer();
mailer.from("build@agiledeveloper.com");
mailer.to("venkats@agiledeveloper.com");
mailer.subject("build notification");
mailer.body("...your code sucks...");
mailer.send();
```

We've all encountered code like this, but it has a couple of smells. First, it's noisy; we had to repeat the mailer so many times. Second, at the end of the call, what do we do with the mailer instance? Can we reuse it for another set of calls, or is it disposable? How do we know?

One answer may be "go read the documentation," but that doesn't help the "put that 'read me' document away and start tinkering with stuff" types among us. Let's design this API so it's more intuitive and fluent.

Using Method Chaining

We discussed two smells: repeated use of mailer reference and unclear object lifetime. Let's address the first smell now.

Rather than repeating the reference, it would be great to continue a conversational state on a context object. We can achieve this using a simple *method chaining* or *cascade method* pattern. In this pattern, rather than having void methods, we make each method return an instance. This returned object is often *this*, the object on which the method is invoked. We use this returned object to build on or chain the subsequent call. Let's evolve the Mailer to use this design; we'll call the new version the MailBuilder. Each method of the class, except the terminal methods like send(), returns a reference instead of being void.

```
designing/fpij/MailBuilder.java
public class MailBuilder {
  public MailBuilder from(final String address) { /*... */; return this; }
  public MailBuilder to(final String address)   { /*... */; return this; }
  public MailBuilder subject(final String line) { /*... */; return this; }
  public MailBuilder body(final String message) { /*... */; return this; }
  public void send() { System.out.println("sending..."); }

  //...
}
```

The new interface will be less noisy to use; we get rid of the repetitive variable name and nicely chain the calls.

designing/fpij/MailBuilder.java

```
new MailBuilder()
  .from("build@agiledeveloper.com")
  .to("venkats@agiledeveloper.com")
  .subject("build notification")
  .body("...it sucks less...")
  .send();
```

We started with a MailBuilder instance and chained the calls to the functions, in sequence, on the instance that the previous call returned. The method chaining, or a *train wreck* as some like to call it, passed the state from one call to the next as we moved through the chain. The terminal method, send() in this example, wrapped up the sequence.

Even though this design reduced the noise, it has a few disadvantages. The new keyword sticks out, reducing the API's fluency and readability. The design does not prevent someone from storing the reference from new and then chaining from that reference. In the latter case, we'd still have the issue with object lifetime, the second smell I mentioned earlier. Also, there are a lot of corner cases—for example, we have to ensure methods like from() are called exactly once.

We need to refine the design further to make it more intuitive and fluent. Let's call our friends, lambda expressions, for help.

Making the API Intuitive and Fluent

Let's evolve the design further. This time we'll combine the method-chaining approach with lambda expressions. We'll call this version of mailer FluentMailer.

designing/fpij/FluentMailer.java

```
public class FluentMailer {
  private FluentMailer() {}

  public FluentMailer from(final String address) { /*... */; return this; }
  public FluentMailer to(final String address)   { /*... */; return this; }
  public FluentMailer subject(final String line) { /*... */; return this; }
  public FluentMailer body(final String message) { /*... */; return this; }

  public static void send(final Consumer<FluentMailer> block) {
    final FluentMailer mailer = new FluentMailer();
    block.accept(mailer);
    System.out.println("sending...");
  }

  //...
}
```

Just like in the method-chaining version, all the nonterminal methods return the instance. In addition, in this version we made the constructor private. This will disallow direct object creation. We also made the terminal method, send(), a static method and it expects a Consumer as a parameter.

Rather than creating an instance, users will now invoke send() and pass a block of code. The send() method will create an instance, yield it to the block, and, upon return, complete any required validations and perform its final *send* operations.

This may feel a bit roundabout, but we removed the smells we discussed earlier. The object's scope is confined within the block, and once we return from the send() method, the reference is gone. We can also benefit from the fluent method chaining within the block, without the sour new keyword sticking out. Let's use this new API in an example.

designing/fpij/FluentMailer.java

```
FluentMailer.send(mailer ->
  mailer.from("build@agiledeveloper.com")
        .to("venkats@agiledeveloper.com")
        .subject("build notification")
        .body("...much better..."));
```

We invoked the send() method and passed a lambda expression to it. Within the lambda expression, we received an instance of the mailer and invoked the desired chain of methods on it.

The instance's scope is fairly easy to see: we get it, work with it, and return it. For that reason, this is also called the *loan pattern.*[4]

From a mundane repetitive interface, we evolved the design to support a fluent interface. This design is quite useful in a number of areas in applications. For example, we can use it to configure mailers, to specify database-connection parameters, or anywhere we need to build a series of states on an instance, but in a controlled manner.

We covered how to create fluent interfaces with lambda expressions, but our discussion of design wouldn't be complete without addressing a pesky issue —exceptions. Let's look at that next.

Dealing with Exceptions

Java programmers are quite opinionated about checked exceptions. Irrespective of how we feel about them, checked exceptions are here to stay and we

---

4.   https://wiki.scala-lang.org/display/SYGN/Loan

have to deal with them. Let's look at some options for working with them in the context of lambda expressions.

In the next example we create a lambda expression that invokes a method that potentially throws a checked exception. We take a list of path names and ask for their canonical path using the getCanonicalPath() method.

```java
public class HandleException {
  public static void main(String[] args) throws IOException {
    Stream.of("/usr", "/tmp")
            .map(path -> new File(path).getCanonicalPath())
            .forEach(System.out::println);
    //Error, this code will not compile
  }
}
```

We've decorated the main() method with the throws clause. However, when we compile this code the Java compiler will report an error:

```
... unreported exception IOException; must be caught or declared to be thrown
        .map(path -> new File(path).getCanonicalPath())
                                                      ^
```

```
1 error
```

The error is directly from within the lambda expression passed to the map() method. This method expects as a parameter an implementation of the Function interface. The apply() method of the Function interface does not specify any checked exceptions. So, our lambda expression that stands in for the abstract method in this example is not permitted to throw any checked exceptions.

We're limited to two options here: we could either handle the exception right there within the lambda expression, or catch it and rethrow it as an unchecked exception. Let's try the first option:

```java
Stream.of("/usr", "/tmp")
        .map(path -> {
          try {
            return new File(path).getCanonicalPath();
          } catch(IOException ex) {
            return ex.getMessage();
          }
        })
        .forEach(System.out::println);
```

In this scenario, if there were an exception, we'd return the exception details instead of the canonical path. Alternatively, to make it easier to identify success versus failure, we could return an object instead of a string. We could design the result object to carry two fields, one with a valid path response and the other with an optional error message.

Instead of handling the exception, we could replace the return within the catch with a `throw new RuntimeException(ex);` and propagate the exception—see *Integrating with the Web Service*, on page 71, for an example of this approach. We can improve the client code's readability quite a bit by creating static helpers for this catch and rethrow.

Transforming from a checked to an unchecked exception and rethrowing may work fine if the calls to the lambda expressions are made sequentially. If the calls are made concurrently from different threads, however, there are a few caveats.

In a concurrent execution, an exception raised within the lambda expressions will be propagated automatically to the calling primary thread. There are two snags: First, this will not terminate or obstruct the execution of other lambda expressions running concurrently. Second, if exceptions are thrown from multiple concurrent executions, only one of them will be reported in the catch block. If the details of all the exceptions are important, it's better to capture those within the lambda expressions and pass them back to the main thread as part of the result.

In the previous example we were limited to the Function interface since the map() method relies on it. When we design our own higher-order functions based on our specific needs, we can more flexibly design the companion functional interfaces to go with it. For example, the next code shows a functional interface whose method specifies a checked exception using the throws clause.

```
resources/fpij/UseInstance.java
@FunctionalInterface
public interface UseInstance<T, X extends Throwable> {
  void accept(T instance) throws X;
}
```

Any method that accepts a parameter of the UseInstance interface will expect and be ready to handle appropriate exceptions or propagate them. We'll take a closer look at this design option in *Using Higher-Order Functions*, on page 92.

The preceding idiom is tailored for lambda expressions that throw exactly one exception—for example, IOException. If the lambda expressions were to throw one of many exceptions, such as IOException or SQLException, then the parametric type X would need to be modeled as the least upper-bound of these exceptions —namely, Exception. If we want to use this to model a lambda expression that throws no exception at all, we'd have to model the parametric type X as RuntimeException.

Exception handling is a sticky issue; when designing and programming with lambda expressions we have to take extra care to handle them properly.

Recap

Lambda expressions are not just a language feature; they turn into a very powerful yet lightweight design tool. Instead of spending the effort to create a hierarchy of interfaces and classes, we can reuse functional interfaces and pass around lambda expressions and method references where possible. This technique can help us easily create delegates to quickly implement the strategy pattern at both the method and the class level. We can also use lambda expressions to implement the decorator pattern. By turning lambda expressions into controlled workhorses, we can create easy-to-read, fluent interfaces as well as configuration details in code. We must take extra care, however, to properly deal with exceptions when working with lambda expressions.

In the next chapter we'll explore a variation of the loan pattern; we'll use lambda expressions to exert greater control when managing object lifetime.

No one is useless in this world who lightens the burden of it to anyone else.

> ➤ *Charles Dickens*

CHAPTER 5

Working with Resources

We may have been led to believe that the JVM automates all garbage collection (GC). It's true that we could let the JVM handle it if we're only using internal resources. However, GC is our responsibility if we use external resources, such as when we connect to databases, open files and sockets, or use native resources.

Java provides a few options to properly clean up resources, but, as we'll see in this chapter, none are as effective as what we can do with lambda expressions. We'll use lambda expressions to implement the *execute around method (EAM)* pattern, which gives us better control over sequencing of operations.[1] Then we'll use this pattern to do even more: manage locks and write exception tests.

Cleaning Up Resources

GC can be a pain to deal with. A company asked me to help debug a problem —one programmer described the issue as "it works fine...most of the time." The application failed during peak usage. It turned out that the code was relying on the finalize() method to release database connections. The JVM figured it had enough memory and opted not to run GC. Since the finalizer was rarely invoked, it led to external resource clogging and the resulting failure.

We need to manage situations like this in a better way, and lambda expressions can help. Let's start with an example problem that involves GC. We'll build the example using a few different approaches, discussing the merits and deficiencies of each. This will help us see the strengths of the final solution using lambda expressions.

---

1.   http://c2.com/cgi/wiki?ExecuteAroundMethod

Peeking into the Problem

We're concerned with external resource cleanup, so let's start with a simple example class that uses a FileWriter to write some messages.

```
resources/fpij/FileWriterExample.java
public class FileWriterExample {
  private final FileWriter writer;

  public FileWriterExample(final String fileName) throws IOException {
    writer = new FileWriter(fileName);
  }
  public void writeStuff(final String message) throws IOException {
    writer.write(message);
  }
  public void finalize() throws IOException {
    writer.close();
  }
  //...
}
```

In the FileWriterExample class's constructor we initialize an instance of FileWriter, giving it the name of a file to write to. In the writeStuff() method we write the given message to the file using the instance of the FileWriter we created. Then, in the finalize() method we clean up the resource, calling close() on it with the hope that it will flush the content to the file and close it.

Let's write a main() method to use this class.

```
resources/fpij/FileWriterExample.java
public static void main(final String[] args) throws IOException {
  final FileWriterExample writerExample =
    new FileWriterExample("peekaboo.txt");
  writerExample.writeStuff("peek-a-boo");
}
```

We created an instance of the FileWriterExample class and invoked the writeStuff() method on it, but if we ran this code, we'd see that the peekaboo.txt file was created but it's empty. The finalizer never ran; the JVM decided it wasn't necessary as there was enough memory. As a result, the file was never closed, and the content we wrote was not flushed from memory.

If we create several instances of the FileWriterExample class in a long-running process we'll end up with several open files. Many of these files will not be closed in a timely manner since the JVM has a lot of memory and sees no reason to run GC.

Let's fix the problem by adding an explicit call to close(), and let's get rid of the finalize() method.

Closing the Resource

When we're done using the instance, we could make an explicit request for its cleanup. Even though the object's memory cleanup is still at the mercy of the JVM GC, we can quickly release the external resources the instance uses. We first need a method to do the cleanup. Let's write that.

resources/fpij/FileWriterExample.java
```java
public void close() throws IOException {
  writer.close();
}
```

In the close() method we simply call the close() method on the FileWriter instance. If we used any other external resources in the FileWriterExample, we can clean them up here, as well. Let's make explicit use of this method in the main() method.

resources/fpij/FileWriterExample.java
```java
final FileWriterExample writerExample =
  new FileWriterExample("peekaboo.txt");

writerExample.writeStuff("peek-a-boo");
writerExample.close();
```

If we run the code now and look into the peekaboo.txt file, we'll see the peek-a-boo message. The code works, but it's far from perfect.

The explicit call to close() cleans up any external resources the instance uses, as soon as we indicate the instance is no longer needed. However, we may not reach the call to the close() method if there was an exception in the code leading up to it. We'll have to do a bit more work to ensure the call to close() happens. Let's take care of that next.

Ensuring Cleanup

We need to ensure the call to close() happens whether or not there's an exception. To achieve this we can wrap the call in a finally block.

resources/fpij/FileWriterExample.java
```java
final FileWriterExample writerExample =
  new FileWriterExample("peekaboo.txt");
try {
  writerExample.writeStuff("peek-a-boo");
} finally {
  writerExample.close();
}
```

This version will ensure resource cleanup even if an exception occurs in the code, but that's a lot of effort and the code is quite smelly. The automatic resource management (ARM) feature, introduced in Java 7, was designed to reduce such smells, as we'll see next.

Using ARM

ARM can reduce the verbosity in the previous example. Rather than using both the try and finally blocks, we can use a special form of the try block with a resource attached to it. Then the Java compiler takes care of automatically inserting the finally block and the call to the close() method.

Let's see how the code would look with ARM; we'll use an instance of a new FileWriterARM class.

resources/fpij/FileWriterARM.java
```
try(final FileWriterARM writerARM = new FileWriterARM("peekaboo.txt")) {
  writerARM.writeStuff("peek-a-boo");

  System.out.println("done with the resource...");
}
```

We created an instance of the class FileWriterARM within the safe haven of the *try-with-resources* form and invoked the writeStuff() method within its block. When we leave the scope of the try block, the close() method is automatically called on the instance/resource managed by this try block. For this to work, the compiler requires the managed resource class to implement the AutoCloseable interface, which has just one method, close().

The rules around AutoCloseable have gone through a few changes in Java 8. First, Stream implements AutoCloseable and as a result all input/output (I/O)-backed streams can be used with try-with-resources. The contract of AutoCloseable has been modified from a strict "the resource *must* be closed" to a more relaxed "the resource *can* be closed." If we're certain that our code uses an I/O resource, then we should use try-with-resources.

Here's the FileWriterARM class used in the previous code.

resources/fpij/FileWriterARM.java
```
public class FileWriterARM implements AutoCloseable {
  private final FileWriter writer;

  public FileWriterARM(final String fileName) throws IOException {
    writer = new FileWriter(fileName);
  }

  public void writeStuff(final String message) throws IOException {
    writer.write(message);
  }
```

```
  public void close() throws IOException {
    System.out.println("close called automatically...");
    writer.close();
  }

  //...
}
```

Let's run the code and look at the peekaboo.txt file and the console for the code's output.

```
done with the resource...
close called automatically...
```

We can see the close() method was called as soon as we left the try block. The instance we created when entering the try block is not accessible beyond the point of leaving the block. The memory that instance uses will be garbage-collected eventually based on the GC strategy the JVM employs.

The previous code using ARM is quite concise and charming, but the programmers have to remember to use it. The code won't complain if we ignore this elegant construct; it will simply create an instance and call methods like writeStuff() outside of any try blocks. If we're looking for a way to really ensure timely cleanup and avoid programmer errors, we have to look beyond ARM, as we'll do next.

Using Lambda Expressions to Clean Up Resources

ARM was a good step in the right direction, but it's not very effective—never trust anything with the word *management* in it, right? Just kidding. Anyone using our class has to figure out that it implements AutoCloseable and remember to use the *try-with-resources* construct. It'd be great if the API we design could guide the programmers and, with the compiler's help, point them in the right direction. We can achieve that quite easily with lambda expressions.

Preparing the Class for Resource Cleanup

We'll design a class, FileWriterEAM, that encapsulates heavy resources that need timely cleanup. In this example we'll use the FileWriter to represent that resource. Let's make both the constructor and the close() methods private—that'll grab the attention of programmers trying to use the class. They can't create an instance directly, and can't invoke the close() on it either. Before we discuss it further, let's implement the design devised so far.

resources/fpij/FileWriterEAM.java

```
public class FileWriterEAM  {
  private final FileWriter writer;

  private FileWriterEAM(final String fileName) throws IOException {
    writer = new FileWriter(fileName);
  }
  private void close() throws IOException {
    System.out.println("close called automatically...");
    writer.close();
  }
  public void writeStuff(final String message) throws IOException {
    writer.write(message);
  }
  //...
}
```

The private constructor and the private close methods are in place, along with
the public method writeStuff().

Using Higher-Order Functions

Since the programmers can't directly create an instance of FileWriterEAM, we
need a factory method for them to use. Unlike the regular factory methods
that create an instance and throw it across the fence, our method will yield
it to users and wait for them to finish their work with it. We'll use the help of
lambda expressions to do this, as we'll see soon. Let's write this method first.

resources/fpij/FileWriterEAM.java

```
public static void use(final String fileName,
  final UseInstance<FileWriterEAM, IOException> block) throws IOException {

  final FileWriterEAM writerEAM = new FileWriterEAM(fileName);
  try {
    block.accept(writerEAM);
  } finally {
    writerEAM.close();
  }
}
```

In the use() method, we receive two parameters, fileName and a reference to an
interface UseInstance (which we haven't defined yet). Within this method we
instantiate FileWriterEAM, and within the safe haven of the try and finally block
we pass the instance to an accept() method of our soon-to-be-created interface.
When the call returns, we invoke the close() method on the instance in the
finally block. Instead of using this construct, we could use ARM within the use()
method. In any case, the users of our class don't have to worry about these
details.

The use() method represents the structure of the *execute around method* pattern. The main action here is the use of the instance within the accept() method, but the creation and cleanup operations nicely surround this call.

Before we can exercise this code, let's take care of the last missing piece, the UseInstance interface.

```
resources/fpij/UseInstance.java
@FunctionalInterface
public interface UseInstance<T, X extends Throwable> {
  void accept(T instance) throws X;
}
```

UseInstance is a functional interface, an ideal candidate for the Java compiler to automatically synthesize from lambda expressions or method references. We marked the interface with the @FunctionalInterface annotation. This is purely optional, but is useful to convey our intent more explicitly. Whether we use this interface or not, the compiler will automatically recognize functional interfaces structurally, as we discussed in *A Little Sugar to Sweeten*, on page 15.

We could have used a java.function.Consumer interface instead of defining our own UseInstance; however, since the method may throw an exception, we needed to indicate that in our interface. Lambda expressions can only throw checked exceptions defined as part of the signature of the abstract method being synthesized (see *Dealing with Exceptions*, on page 83). We created the UseInstance interface so that the accept() method can accept an instance of a generic type; in this example, we tied it down to an instance of a concrete FileWriterEAM. We also designed it so this method implementation could potentially throw a generic exception X—again, in this example tied to the concrete class IOException.

Using the Design for Instance Cleanup

As the class's designers, we put in a bit more effort than simply implementing the AutoCloseable interface. This extra investment on our part quickly will pay recurring dividends: each time programmers use our class, they'll get instant resource cleanup, as we can see here:

```
resources/fpij/FileWriterEAM.java
FileWriterEAM.use("eam.txt", writerEAM -> writerEAM.writeStuff("sweet"));
```

First, our class's users can't create an instance directly. This prevents them from creating code that would postpone the resource cleanup beyond its expiration point (unless they go through extreme measures, such as using reflection, to defeat the mechanism). Since the compiler will prevent calls to the constructor or the close() method, the programmers will quickly figure out the benefit of the use() method, which yields an instance for their use. To invoke use(), they can use the short-and-sweet syntax that lambda expressions provide, as we saw in the previous code.

Let's run this version of code and look at the eam.txt file it creates.

sweet

Let's also glance at the console for the output from the code.

close called automatically...

We can see that the file has the proper output and that the resource cleanup happened automatically.

In the example we use the given instance writerEAM for just one call within the lambda expression. If we have to perform more operations with it, we can send it off to other functions as an argument. We can also perform a few operations on it, right within the lambda expression, by using multiline syntax.

```
resources/fpij/FileWriterEAM.java
FileWriterEAM.use("eam2.txt", writerEAM -> {
    writerEAM.writeStuff("how");
    writerEAM.writeStuff("sweet");
  });
```

We can place multiple lines of code within a lambda expression by wrapping them in a {} block. If the lambda expression is expected to return a result, be sure to place a return at the appropriate expression. The Java compiler gives us the flexibility to write just one line or wrap multiple lines, but we should keep lambda expressions short.

Long methods are bad, but long lambda expressions are evil—we would lose the benefit of code that's concise, easy to understand, and simple to maintain. Instead of writing long lambda expressions, we should move the code into other methods and then use method references for them if possible, or invoke them from within a lambda expression.

In this example the UseInstance's accept() is a void method. If we were interested in returning some results to the caller of the use() method, we'd have to modify this method's signature to place an appropriate return type, such as a generic parameter R. If we were to make this change, then the UseInstance would be more like the Function<U, R> interface than like the Consumer<T> interface. We'd also have to change the use() method to propagate the return results from the modified apply() method.

We used lambda expressions to implement the *execute around method* pattern. We can benefit from this pattern when designing classes that require prompt cleanup of resources. Rather than shifting the burden to our class's users, we put in a bit more effort that made their lives much easier and the behavior of our code a lot more consistent.

This pattern is not restricted to the cleanup of resources. For me, the pattern came to life on a project where my team had to perform operations within the bounds of transactions. Rather than creating and managing transactions all over the code, we wrapped them into a nice runWithinTransaction() method. The method's callers received a transaction instance, and when they returned the method took care of checking the status as well as performing actions such as committing or rolling back the transaction and logging.

We used lambda expressions and the *execute around method* pattern to manage resources. Next we'll use it to manage locks.

Managing Locks

Locks play a critical part in concurrent Java applications. In this section we'll use lambda expressions to gain finer control over locks and open the doors to unit-test the proper locking of critical sections.

synchronized is an age-old keyword used to provide mutual exclusion. A synchronized block of code, such as synchronized { ... }, is a realization of the *execute around method* pattern. This pattern has been around since Java 1.0, but it was restricted and bound to the synchronized keyword in Java. Lambda expressions have now unleashed this pattern's power.

synchronized has some shortcomings—see *Java Concurrency in Practice [Goe06]*, by Brian Goetz, and *Programming Concurrency on the JVM [Sub11]*. First, it's hard to time out a call to synchronized, and this can increase the chance of deadlocks and livelocks. Second, it's hard to mock out synchronized, and that makes it really hard to unit-test to see if code adheres to proper thread safety.

To address these concerns, the Lock interface, along with a few implementations such as ReentrantLock, was introduced in Java 5. The Lock interface gives us better control to lock, unlock, check if a lock is available, and easily time out if a lock is not gained within a certain time span. Because this is an interface, it's easy to mock up its implementation for the sake of unit testing.[2]

---

2. https://www.agiledeveloper.com/presentations/TestDrivingMultiThreadedCode.zip

There's one caveat to the Lock interface—unlike its counterpart synchronized, it requires explicit locking and unlocking. This means we not only have to remember to unlock, but to do so within the finally block. From our discussions so far in this chapter, we can see lambda expressions and the *execute around method* pattern helping out quite a bit here.

Let's first look at a piece of code that uses a Lock.

resources/fpij/Locking.java
```
public class Locking {
  Lock lock = new ReentrantLock(); //or mock

  protected void setLock(final Lock mock) {
    lock = mock;
  }

  public void doOp1() {
    lock.lock();
    try {
      //...critical code...
    } finally {
      lock.unlock();
    }
  }
  //...
}
```

We're using a Lock lock field to share the lock between methods of this class. However, the task of locking—for example, within the doOp1() method—leaves a lot to be desired. It's verbose, error prone, and hard to maintain. Let's turn to lambda expressions for help, and create a small class to manage the lock.

resources/fpij/Locker.java
```
public class Locker {
  public static void runLocked(Lock lock, Runnable block) {
    lock.lock();

    try {
      block.run();
    } finally {
      lock.unlock();
    }
  }
}
```

This class absorbs the pain of working with the Lock interface so the rest of the code benefits. We can use the runLocked() method in code to wrap critical sections.

resources/fpij/Locking.java
```java
public void doOp2() {
  runLocked(lock, () -> {/*...critical code ... */});
}

public void doOp3() {
  runLocked(lock, () -> {/*...critical code ... */});
}

public void doOp4() {
  runLocked(lock, () -> {/*...critical code ... */});
}
```

The methods are quite concise, and they use the static method runLocked() of the Locker helper class we created (we'd need an import static Locker.runLocked for this code to compile). Lambda expressions come to our assistance once more.

We saw how the *execute around method* pattern helps to make the code concise and less error prone, but the elegance and conciseness should help remove the ceremony, not hide what's essential. When designing with lambda expressions, we should ensure that the intent of the code and its consequences are clearly visible. Also, when creating lambda expressions that capture local state, we must be aware of the restrictions we discussed in *Are there restrictions to lexical scoping?*, on page 31.

Let's look at one more benefit the *execute around method* pattern offers, in unit testing with JUnit.

Creating Concise Exception Tests

When Java 5 annotations were introduced, JUnit was quick to use them. Overall this has been a benefit, but one use in particular, the convenience of exception tests, leads to terse rather than concise code. Let's understand the issues and then resolve them using—good guess—lambda expressions. We will see here that lambda expressions are not just another language feature; they alter the way we think and design applications.

Suppose we're driving the design of a class, RodCutter, through unit tests and we expect a method maxProfit() to throw an exception if the argument is zero. Let's look at a few ways we can write the exception tests for it.

Exception Test with try and catch

Here's the test for the maxProfit() method with try and catch to check for exceptions.

```
resources/fpij/RodCutterTest.java
@Test public void VerboseExceptionTest() {
  rodCutter.setPrices(prices);
  try {
    rodCutter.maxProfit(0);
    fail("Expected exception for zero length");
  } catch(RodCutterException ex) {
    assertTrue("expected", true);
  }
}
```

That's quite verbose and it may take some effort to understand, but this code is quite specific about what's expected to fail: the call to the maxProfit() method.

Exception Test Using Annotation

We may be tempted to attack the verbosity with annotation.

```
resources/fpij/RodCutterTest.java
@Test(expected = RodCutterException.class)
public void TerseExceptionTest() {
  rodCutter.setPrices(prices);
  rodCutter.maxProfit(0);
}
```

The code is short but deceptive—it's terse. It tells us that the test should pass if the exception RodCutterException is received, but it fails to ensure that the method that raised that exception is maxProfit(). If the setPrices() method threw that exception, due to some code change, then this test will continue to pass, but for the wrong reason. A good test should pass only for the right reasons —this test deceives us.

Using Lambda Expressions for Exception Tests

Let's use lambda expressions to look for exceptions. We'll manually create the code for this in a TestHelper class, but if and when JUnit supports this natively we won't have to write such a class.

```
resources/fpij/TestHelper.java
public class TestHelper {
  public static <X extends Throwable> Throwable assertThrows(
    final Class<X> exceptionClass, final Runnable block) {

    try {
      block.run();
    } catch(Throwable ex) {
      if(exceptionClass.isInstance(ex))
        return ex;
    }
```

```
      fail("Failed to throw expected exception ");
      return null;
    }
}
```

In the TestHelper we wrote a static method assertThrows() that expects an exception class and a block of code to run. It exercises the block of code, and examines the exception the code throws. If no exception was thrown or if an exception other than the type given in the first parameter was received, the call will fail using the JUnit fail() method.

Let's use this helper to create a concise test.

resources/fpij/RodCutterTest.java
```
@Test
public void ConciseExceptionTest() {
  rodCutter.setPrices(prices);
  assertThrows(RodCutterException.class, () -> rodCutter.maxProfit(0));
}
```

This test is fine grained—it will pass only if the method maxProfit() throws the expected exception.

Exercising the Tests

We have three versions of exception tests so far; let's review them.

resources/fpij/RodCutterTest.java
```
@Test public void VerboseExceptionTest() {
  rodCutter.setPrices(prices);
  try {
    rodCutter.maxProfit(0);
    fail("Expected exception for zero length");
  } catch(RodCutterException ex) {
    assertTrue("expected", true);
  }
}

@Test(expected = RodCutterException.class)
public void TerseExceptionTest() {
  rodCutter.setPrices(prices);
  rodCutter.maxProfit(0);
}

@Test
public void ConciseExceptionTest() {
  rodCutter.setPrices(prices);
  assertThrows(RodCutterException.class, () -> rodCutter.maxProfit(0));
}
```

All these tests are checking whether the maxProfit() method throws an exception. Let's implement minimal code in the RodCutter class to make the tests pass.

```
resources/fpij/RodCutter.java
public class RodCutter {
  public void setPrices(final List<Integer> prices) {
  }
  public int maxProfit(final int length) {
    if (length == 0) throw new RodCutterException();

    return 0;
  }
}
```

The maxProfit() method throws an exception if the value of the length parameter is zero, which is exactly what the tests are checking for. Let's look at the result of running the tests.

```
...
Time: ...

OK (3 tests)
```

All three tests passed, indicating that the maxProfit() blew up as expected.

All the tests achieve the same goal, but the last concise version is better than the others; one change to the setPrice() method will show us why.

```
resources/fpij/RodCutter.java
public void setPrices(final List<Integer> prices) {
    throw new RodCutterException();
}
```

The setPrice() method, which is called in each of the tests, now abruptly throws the RodCutterException exception. Since the tests are expecting the method maxProfit() to throw a specific exception, any other behavior in the invoked code should trigger an alert. Good tests would fail now due to the code change we made; poor tests will quietly pass. Let's run the tests to see how they perform.

```
.E.E.
Time: ...
There were 2 errors:
...
```

The change to the setPrices() method should have caused all three tests to fail, but only two failed, as we can see from the output. If we examine the full output of the tests, we'll find the culprit: the terse version using the annotation facility for the exception test.

We want to avoid the terse version, as it is plain wrong. We're now limited to the other two versions that behave properly. We can narrow the choice further to the concise version—no need to write more code when fewer lines of readable code can accomplish the same thing.

We saw how lambda expressions help us write tests that target specific methods for the expected exception, and that helps us create concise, easy-to-read, less error-prone tests.

Recap

We can't totally rely on automatic garbage collection, especially when our applications use external resources. The *execute around method* pattern can help us gain finer control over the flow of execution, and release external resources. Lambda expressions are a good fit to implement this pattern. In addition to controlling the object lifetime, we can use this pattern to better manage locks and to write concise exception tests. This can lead to more deterministic execution of code, timely cleanup of heavyweight resources, and fewer errors.

We managed resources in this chapter. In the next we'll use lambda expressions to delay execution of some parts of code as a way to make the programs more efficient.

Progress is made by lazy men looking for easier ways to do things.

> ➤ *Robert A. Heinlein*

CHAPTER 6

Being Lazy

In Java we often execute code eagerly. The arguments are evaluated right at the time of method calls, for example. There's a good reason for that; eager code is easy to write and to reason about. But delaying commitments until the last responsible moment is a good agile practice. When executing code, we can gain in performance by being just a little lazy. Eager is simple, but lazy is efficient. Now we can easily be lazy and make things simple and efficient.

If we use heavyweight objects in a program, we want to postpone creating them. Certainly we'd delay running any expensive computations until we really need them. Paradoxically, laziness often requires effort, and this creates an impediment. After all, who wants to work hard to be lazy? In Java 8 we don't have to; we can relax because lambda expressions make running our programs both lazy and fast.

In this chapter we start with a task to postpone the creation of a heavyweight object, then we turn some eager computations into lazy evaluations. As the last task we look at creating infinite lazy sequences by exploiting the laziness built into Streams. The tricks from this chapter can help our programs run faster, our code become more concise, and us look smarter.

Delayed Initialization

In object-oriented programming we ensure that objects are well constructed before any method calls. We encapsulate, ensure proper state transitions, and preserve the object's invariants. This works well most of the time, but when parts of an object's internals are heavyweight resources, we'll benefit if we postpone creating them. This can speed up object creation, and the program doesn't expend any effort creating things that may not be used.

The design decision to postpone creating part of an object should not burden the object's users—it should be seamless. Let's explore some ways to design lazy initialization.

A Familiar Approach

In the following example, we will craft a way to delay the creation of a heavyweight instance. Then we'll improve on the design.

Let's start with a Holder class that needs some heavyweight resources. Creating an instance of this class may take significant time and memory due to the resources it depends on. To address this we can move the heavyweight resources into another class—say, Heavy. Then an instance of Holder will keep a reference to an instance of Heavy and route calls to it as appropriate.

Let's create the Heavy class.

```
lazy/fpij/Heavy.java
public class Heavy {
  public Heavy() { System.out.println("Heavy created"); }

  public String toString() { return "quite heavy"; }
}
```

This class represents a hypothetical heavyweight resource. In its constructor we print a message to tell us when it's created. Let's use an instance of this class in the first trial version of the Holder class, named HolderNaive.

```
lazy/fpij/HolderNaive.java
public class HolderNaive {
  private Heavy heavy;

  public HolderNaive() {
    System.out.println("Holder created");
  }

  public Heavy getHeavy() {
    if(heavy == null) {
      heavy = new Heavy();
    }

    return heavy;
  }

//...
```

At first glance this code appears quite simple. We created a null reference, heavy, and assigned it to a proper instance on the first call to the getHeavy()

method. Let's use this class to create an instance of HolderNaive and see if it postpones the creation of the Heavy instance.

```
lazy/fpij/HolderNaive.java
final HolderNaive holder = new HolderNaive();
System.out.println("deferring heavy creation...");
System.out.println(holder.getHeavy());
System.out.println(holder.getHeavy());
```

This is the code's output:

```
Holder created
deferring heavy creation...
Heavy created
quite heavy
quite heavy
```

That appears to work. The solution is familiar, but it's also a rather simplistic solution that fails thread safety. Let's work through it.

Providing Thread Safety

For an instance of HolderNaive, the dependent instance of Heavy is created on the first call to the getHeavy() method. On subsequent calls to this method, the already created instance will be returned. That's exactly what we want, but there's a catch. This code suffers from a race condition.

If two or more threads call the getHeavy() method at the same time, then we could end up with multiple Heavy instances, potentially one per thread. This side effect is undesirable. Let's fix it.

```
public synchronized Heavy getHeavy() {
  if(heavy == null) {
    heavy = new Heavy();
  }

  return heavy;
}
```

We marked getHeavy() with the synchronized keyword to ensure mutual exclusion. If two or more threads call this method concurrently, due to mutual exclusion only one will be allowed to enter and the others will queue up for their turn. The first one to enter into the method will create the instance. When subsequent threads enter this method they will see that the instance already exists, and will simply return it.

We averted the race condition, but the solution created another negative impact. Every call to the getHeavy() method now has to endure the synchronization overhead; the calling threads have to cross the memory barrier (see Brian

Goetz's *Java Concurrency in Practice [Goe06]*) even if there are no concurrently competing threads.

In fact, the possibility of the race condition is so short lived it can happen only when the heavy reference is first being assigned, and the synchronization approach is a rather heavy-handed solution. We need thread safety until the reference is first created, and free unhindered access to the reference after that. We'll achieve this by using David Wheeler's advice: "Any problem in computer science can be solved with another level of indirection."[1]

Adding a Level of Indirection

The indirection we'll add in this example comes from a Supplier<T> class. This is a functional interface in the JDK, with one abstract method named get() that returns an instance. In other words, this is a factory that keeps on giving without expecting anything as input, kind of like a mother's love.

In the most rudimentary form a Supplier will return an instance. For example, we could implement Supplier<Heavy> to return an instance of Heavy, like so:

```
Supplier<Heavy> supplier = () -> new Heavy();
```

Alternatively, we could use a constructor reference instead of the traditional new syntax to instantiate an instance. A constructor reference is much like a method reference, except it's a reference to a constructor instead of a method. We can use a constructor reference anywhere a lambda expression does nothing more than instantiate an instance. Let's look at an example with a constructor reference.

```
Supplier<Heavy> supplier = Heavy::new;
```

We took a look at what a Supplier can do for us, but we need something more than this simple form. We need to postpone and cache the instance. We can do that by moving the instance creation to another function, as we see next, in the final version of the Holder class.

lazy/fpij/Holder.java
```
public class Holder {
  private Supplier<Heavy> heavy = () -> createAndCacheHeavy();

  public Holder() {
    System.out.println("Holder created");
  }

  public Heavy getHeavy() {
```

1.　http://en.wikipedia.org/wiki/David_Wheeler_(computer_scientist)

```
      return heavy.get();
    }
    //...
}
```

The field heavy in this version is an instance of the Supplier<Heavy>. We assign it to a lambda expression and the Java compiler synthesizes from it an instance with the expected get() method. The implementation simply routes the call to a createAndCacheHeavy() method, which we'll implement soon. The getHeavy() method returns the same thing the Supplier's get method returns.

When an instance of Holder is created, as we can see, an instance of Heavy is not created. This design achieves the goal of lazy initialization. We also need a non-draconian solution to thread safety. This is where the createAndCacheHeavy() method comes in.

Let's first look at the code for this method.

lazy/fpij/Holder.java
```
private synchronized Heavy createAndCacheHeavy() {
  class HeavyFactory implements Supplier<Heavy> {
    private final Heavy heavyInstance = new Heavy();

    public Heavy get() { return heavyInstance; }
  }

  if(!HeavyFactory.class.isInstance(heavy)) {
    heavy = new HeavyFactory();
  }

  return heavy.get();
}
```

We'll mark this method synchronized so threads calling this method concurrently will be mutually exclusive. But within this method, on the first call we quickly replace the Supplier reference heavy with a direct supplier, HeavyFactory, that will return an instance of Heavy. Let's see how this adequately solves thread safety.

Let's consider a scenario in which a new instance of Holder has just been created. Let's assume two threads invoke the getHeavy() method concurrently, followed by a third thread calling this method much later. When the first two threads call the default supplier's get() method in the Holder, the createAndCacheHeavy() method will let one of them through and make the other wait. The first thread to enter will check if heavy is an instance of the HeavyFactory. Since it is not the default Supplier, this thread will replace heavy with an instance of HeavyFactory. Finally it returns the Heavy instance that this HeavyFactory holds.

The second concurrent thread to enter will again check if heavy is an instance of HeavyFactory, and will bypass the creation. It would simply return the same instance that first thread returned. Here we assume Heavy itself is thread safe, and we're only focusing on the thread safety of Holder.

We've taken care of the race condition, but since the instance has been created lazily, we no longer need to be so protective. Now that heavy has been replaced with HeavyFactory, subsequent calls to the getHeavy() method will go directly to the HeavyFactory's get() method and will not incur any synchronization overhead.

We designed lazy initialization and, at the same time, avoided null checks. Furthermore, we ensured the thread safety of the lazy instance creation. This is a simple, lightweight implementation of the *virtual proxy* pattern. Next we'll use lambda expressions to postpone function evaluations.

Lazy Evaluations

In the previous section we delayed creation of heavyweight objects to make code execution faster. We'll explore that further in this section to delay running methods, and use that approach to improve our designs. The main objective is to reduce the execution of code to the bare minimum—especially the expensive code—and speed up the execution.

Java already uses lazy execution when evaluating logical operations. For example, in fn1() || fn2(), the call fn2() is never performed if fn1() returns a boolean true. Likewise, if we replace the || with &&, the call to fn2() never happens if fn1() returns a boolean false. Programs benefit from this short-circuiting; we avoid unnecessary evaluation of expressions or functions, and that can help improve performance. Often we rely on such short-circuiting for code correctness, as well.

While Java uses lazy or normal order when evaluating logical operators, it uses eager or applicative order when evaluating method arguments. All the arguments to methods are fully evaluated before a method is invoked. If the method doesn't use all of the passed arguments, the program has wasted time and effort executing them. We can use lambda expressions to postpone the execution of select arguments.

The Java compiler evaluates lambda expressions and method references in the argument list at the called location. The invocation of these, however, is postponed until they are explicitly called from within the methods they're passed to. We can take advantage of this behavior to delay or even avoid method invocation by embedding calls to them within lambda expressions.

We can't seamlessly wrap arbitrary arguments into lambda expressions, however. We have to explicitly design for it, as we'll see here.

Quite a few methods in the JDK—including methods on the Stream class—do lazy evaluation. For instance, the filter() method may not invoke the Predicate, passed as an argument, on all the elements in the target collection.

We can design lazy evaluation of arguments to methods by turning the parameters into functional interfaces. Let's work that approach into an example to get a feel for the design.

Starting with Eager Evaluation

In the example here, methods take significant time to run. We'll call them eagerly and then alter the design to improve speed.

Let's start with a method evaluate() that takes quite a bit of time and resources to run.

```
lazy/fpij/Evaluation.java
public class Evaluation {
  public static boolean evaluate(final int value) {
    System.out.println("evaluating ..." + value);
    simulateTimeConsumingOp(2000);
    return value > 100;
  }
  //...
}
```

A call to evaluate() would take a couple of seconds to run, so we definitely want to postpone any unnecessary calls. Let's create a method, eagerEvaluator(), which is like almost any method we write in Java: all of its arguments will be evaluated before its call.

```
lazy/fpij/Evaluation.java
public static void eagerEvaluator(
  final boolean input1, final boolean input2) {
  System.out.println("eagerEvaluator called...");
  System.out.println("accept?: " + (input1 && input2));
}
```

The method takes two boolean parameters. Within the method we perform a logical *and* operation on the parameters. Sadly, it's too late to benefit from the lazy evaluation this operation automatically provides since the arguments are evaluated well before we enter this method.

Let's invoke eagerEvaluator() and pass as arguments the results of two evaluate() method calls.

lazy/fpij/Evaluation.java
```
eagerEvaluator(evaluate(1), evaluate(2));
```

If we run this code we'll see both the calls to evaluate() execute well before we enter the eagerEvaluator() method.

```
evaluating ...1
evaluating ...2
eagerEvaluator called...
accept?: false
```

This would take at least four seconds to run because of the cumulative delay from the calls to the evaluate() method. We'll improve on that next.

Designing for Lazy Evaluation

If we know that some arguments may not be used during the execution of a method, we can design the method's interface to facilitate the delayed execution of some or all arguments. The arguments can be evaluated on demand, like in this lazyEvaluator() method:

lazy/fpij/Evaluation.java
```
public static void lazyEvaluator(
  final Supplier<Boolean> input1, final Supplier<Boolean> input2) {
  System.out.println("lazyEvaluator called...");
  System.out.println("accept?: " + (input1.get() && input2.get()));
}
```

Rather than taking two boolean parameters, the method receives references to the Supplier instances. This JDK functional interface will return an instance, Boolean in this case, in response to a call to its get() method. The logical *and* operation we use within the lazyEvaluator() method will invoke the get() methods only on demand.

If we pass two calls to evaluate() as arguments to the lazyEvaluator() method, the second will be evaluated only if the first call returned a boolean true. Let's run the method to see this.

lazy/fpij/Evaluation.java
```
lazyEvaluator(() -> evaluate(1), () -> evaluate(2));
```

Each Supplier makes a call to the evaluate() method, but not until the lazyEvaluator() method is invoked. The evaluation is lazy and optional, determined by the flow of execution within the lazyEvaluator() method. We can see this delayed evaluation in the output when we run the code.

```
lazyEvaluator called...
evaluating ...1
accept?: false
```

The arguments are not evaluated before we enter the lazyEvaluator() method. The second call to evaluate() was skipped in this version. This example call of lazyEvaluator() takes only about two seconds, whereas the previous call to eagerEvaluator() took about four seconds.

We saw the cost savings of the lazy evaluation. This technique is quite helpful when we have to evaluate a large number of methods or if method evaluations are time/resource consuming.

This technique can significantly boost performance, but its disadvantage is that it burdens the caller with packaging the calls in a lambda expression. Sure, lambda expressions are concise, but they're a hindrance compared to the usual way of passing arguments. In some contexts we may be able to use method references instead of lambda expressions, and this can make the code a bit more concise and ease the burden a little.

The lazy solutions so far have helped us make code more efficient. Next we'll use it purely for convenience.

Leveraging the Laziness of Streams

In previous chapters we've seen the facilities that the new Stream interface offers, but so far we haven't discussed one of their most salient features—they're really lazy, in a good way. The lazy evaluation of Streams is quite powerful. First, we don't have to do anything special to derive their benefits. In fact, we've used them many times already! Second, they can postpone not just one, but a sequence of evaluations so that only the most essential parts of the logic are evaluated, and only when needed. Let's look at how lazy Streams are and how we benefit from that.

Intermediate and Terminal Operations

Streams have two types of methods: *intermediate* and *terminal*, which work together. The secret behind their laziness is that we chain multiple intermediate operations followed by a terminal operation.

Methods like map() and filter() are intermediate; calls to them return immediately and the lambda expressions provided to them are not evaluated right away. The core behavior of these methods is cached for later execution and no real work is done when they're called. The cached behavior is run when one of the terminal operations, like findFirst() and reduce(), is called. Not all the cached code is executed, however, and the computation will complete as soon as the desired result is found. Let's look at an example to understand this better.

Suppose we're given a collection of names and are asked to print in all caps the first name that is only three letters long. We can use Stream's functional-style methods to achieve this. But first let's create a few helper methods.

lazy/fpij/LazyStreams.java

```java
public class LazyStreams {
    private static int length(final String name) {
        System.out.println("getting length for " + name);
        return name.length();
    }
    private static String toUpper(final String name ) {
        System.out.println("converting to uppercase: " + name);
        return name.toUpperCase();
    }
    //...
}
```

The two helper methods simply print the parameters they receive before returning the expected results. We wrote these methods to take a peek at the intermediate operations in the code we'll write next.

lazy/fpij/LazyStreams.java

```java
public static void main(final String[] args) {
    List<String> names = Arrays.asList("Brad", "Kate", "Kim", "Jack", "Joe",
        "Mike", "Susan", "George", "Robert", "Julia", "Parker", "Benson");

    final String firstNameWith3Letters =
        names.stream()
            .filter(name -> length(name) == 3)
            .map(name -> toUpper(name))
            .findFirst()
            .get();

    System.out.println(firstNameWith3Letters);
}
```

We started with a list of names, transformed it into a Stream, filtered out only names that are three letters long, converted the selected names to all caps, and picked the first name from that set.

At first glance it appears the code is doing a lot of work transforming collections, but it's deceptively lazy; it didn't do any more work than absolutely essential. Let's take a look.

Method Evaluation Order

It would help to read the code from right to left, or bottom up, to see what's really going on here. Each step in the call chain will do only enough work to ensure that the terminal operation in the chain completes. This behavior is in direct contrast to the usual eager evaluation, but is efficient.

If the code were eager, the filter() method would have first gone through all dozen names in the collection to create a list of two names, Kim and Joe, whose length is three (letters). The subsequent call to the map() method would have then evaluated the two names. The findFirst() method finally would have picked the first element of this reduced list. We can visualize this hypothetical eager order of evaluation in the next figure.

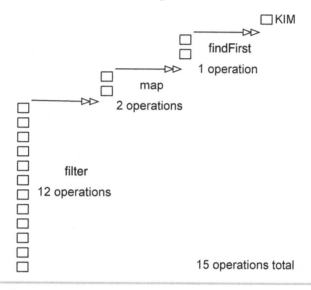

Figure 6—Hypothetical eager evaluation of operations

However, both the filter() and map() methods are lazy to the bone. As the execution goes through the chain, the filter() and map() methods store the lambda expressions and pass on a façade to the next call in the chain. The evaluations start only when findFirst(), a terminal operation, is called.

The order of evaluation is different as well, as we see in Figure 7, *Actual lazy evaluation of operations*, on page 114. The filter() method does not plow through all the elements in the collection in one shot. Instead, it runs until it finds the first element that satisfies the condition given in the attached lambda expression. As soon as it finds an element, it passes that to the next method in the chain. This next method, map() in this example, does its part on the given input and passes it down the chain. When the evaluation reaches the end, the terminal operation checks to see if it has received the result it's looking for.

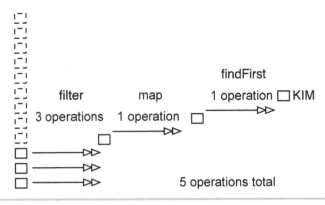

Figure 7—Actual lazy evaluation of operations

If the terminal operation got what it needed, the computation of the chain terminates. If the terminal operation is not satisfied, it will ask for the chain of operations to be carried out for more elements in the collection.

By examining the logic of this sequencing of operations, we can see that the execution will iterate over only essential elements in the collection. We can see evidence of this behavior by running the code.

```
getting length for Brad
getting length for Kate
getting length for Kim
converting to uppercase: Kim
KIM
```

From the output we can see that most of the elements in the example list were not evaluated once the candidate name we're looking for was found.

The logical sequence of operations we saw in the previous example is achieved under the hood in the JDK using a *fusing* operation—all the functions in the intermediate operations are fused together into one function that is evaluated for each element, as appropriate, until the terminal operation is satisfied. In essence, there's only one pass on the data—filtering, mapping, and selecting the element all happen in one shot.

Peeking into the Laziness

Writing the series of operations as a chain is the preferred and natural way in Java 8. But to really see that the lazy evaluations didn't start until we reached the terminal operation, let's break the chain from the previous code into steps.

```
lazy/fpij/LazyStreams.java
Stream<String> namesWith3Letters =
  names.stream()
      .filter(name -> length(name) == 3)
      .map(name -> toUpper(name));

System.out.println("Stream created, filtered, mapped...");
System.out.println("ready to call findFirst...");

final String firstNameWith3Letters =
  namesWith3Letters.findFirst()
                   .get();

System.out.println(firstNameWith3Letters);
```

We transformed the collection into a stream, filtered the values, and then mapped the resulting collection. Then, separately, we called the terminal operation. Let's run the code to see the sequence of evaluation.

```
Stream created, filtered, mapped...
ready to call findFirst...
getting length for Brad
getting length for Kate
getting length for Kim
converting to uppercase: Kim
KIM
```

From the output we can clearly see that the intermediate operations delayed their real work until the last responsible moment, when the terminal operation was invoked. And even then, they only did the minimum work necessary to satisfy the terminal operation. Pretty efficient, eh?

This example helped us uncover Stream's true power. Next we'll use Streams to create infinite collections.

Creating Infinite, Lazy Collections

Infinite collections can make the code to create a growing series, like the Fibonacci numbers, clearer and easier to express. But from our experience in Java, we might think a series can't be infinite due to practical memory limits. The laziness of Streams comes in again here.

In Java, collections are still required to be finite but streams can be infinite. We'll see here how laziness becomes an essential workhorse to make infinite streams possible. We'll use them to create highly expressive, easy-to-understand code to produce an infinitely growing series.

A Desperate Attempt

We'll use a series of prime numbers, *2, 3, 5, 7,...* as an example to explore the concepts here. Let's first create a helper function to determine if a number is prime.

```
public static boolean isPrime(final int number) {
  return number > 1 &&
    IntStream.rangeClosed(2, (int) Math.sqrt(number))
             .noneMatch(divisor -> number % divisor == 0);
}
```

A number greater than 1 is prime if it's not divisible by any number between 2 and its square root. Normally we would use an external iterator to search for a divisor in that range. Instead, we use more Java 8 goodness here—the rangeClosed() static method of the new IntStream interface.

The *closed* suffix in the method name emphasizes that the range of values will include the second parameter. For example, rangeClosed(1, 10) will return the range of values 1, 2,..., 10 packed into a Stream. In contrast, the range() method, also a static method in the interface, will return a range of values, up to (but not including) the value in the second parameter.

In the isPrime() method, we use the short and sweet noneMatch() method on the stream returned by the rangeClosed() method. The noneMatch() method takes a Predicate as its parameter and we use this to determine if there's a divisor for the given number. The noneMatch() method will yield a boolean true if the lambda expression returned false for all values in the range—that is, if there are no divisors.

On our first attempt, we'll use the isPrime() method to create a series of prime numbers starting at any given number.

```
//don't try this at the office
public static List<Integer> primes(final int number) {
  if(isPrime(number))
    return concat(number, primes(number + 1));
  else
    return primes(number + 1);
}
```

If a given number is prime we include it in the list of primes that follows the number. Otherwise, we omit it and move on to get that list.

Hold your tweets; no, your humble author has not gone mad—that code is enticingly elegant but, sadly, won't work. If we implement the concat() method and run the code, we'll enter into a never-ending recursion and end up with a java.lang.StackOverflowError.

Let's drill into the code just a bit more to see if we can salvage anything from it. The StackOverflowError is from the recursive calls to the primes() method. If we can be lazy about this call, then we won't run into issues.

Reaching for the Stars

Earlier we saw how lazy Streams are. They don't do any real work until we ask them for the results—kinda like my kids. We can rely on that laziness to easily create a lazy, infinite collection.

When we create a Stream, from a collection or though other means, we quickly receive a façade that has the potential to return an infinite list. But it's wickedly clever; it returns to us only as many elements as we ask for, producing the elements just in time. We can use that capability to express an infinite collection and generate as many (finite) elements as we like from that list. Let's see how.

The Stream interface has a static method iterate() that can create an infinite Stream. It takes two parameters, a *seed* value to start the collection, and an instance of a UnaryOperator interface, which is the supplier of data in the collection. The Stream the iterate() method returns will postpone creating the elements until we ask for them using a terminating method. To get the first element, for example, we could call the findFirst() method. To get ten elements we could call the limit() method on the Stream, like so: limit(10).

Let's see how all these ideas shape up in code.

```
lazy/fpij/Primes.java
public class Primes {
  private static int primeAfter(final int number) {
    if(isPrime(number + 1))
      return number + 1;
    else
      return primeAfter(number + 1);
  }

  public static List<Integer> primes(final int fromNumber, final int count) {
    return Stream.iterate(primeAfter(fromNumber - 1), Primes::primeAfter)
                 .limit(count)
                 .collect(Collectors.<Integer>toList());
  }
  //...
}
```

We first defined a convenience method, primeAfter(), that returns a prime number that's after the given number. If the number next to the given number is prime, it is immediately returned; otherwise, the method recursively asks for the prime number that follows. The code that deals with the infinite series is in the primes() method. It's quite short for what it does; the real complexity is hidden within the iterate() method and the Stream.

The primes() method will create an infinite series of prime numbers, starting with the first prime greater than or equal to the number given as parameter. In the call to the iterate() method, the first parameter provides the seed for the infinite series. If the given number is prime, it's used as the seed. Otherwise the first prime after the number is used. The second parameter, a method reference, stands in for a UnaryOperator that takes in a parameter and returns a value. In this example, since we refer to the primeAfter() method, it takes in a number and returns a prime after the number.

The result of the call to the iterate() method is a Stream that caches the UnaryOperator it's given. When we ask for a particular number of elements, and only then, the Stream will feed the current element (the given seed value is used as the first element) to the cached UnaryOperator to get the next element, and then feed that element back to the UnaryOperator to get the subsequent element. This sequence will repeat as many times as necessary to get the number of elements we asked for, as we see in the next figure.

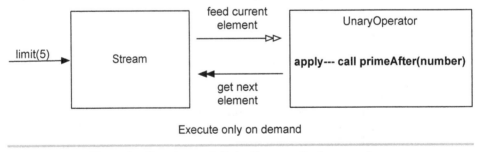

Figure 8—Creating an infinite Stream of prime numbers

Let's call the primes() method first to get ten primes starting at 1, and then five primes starting at 100.

```
lazy/fpij/Primes.java
System.out.println("10 primes from 1: " + primes(1, 10));

System.out.println("5 primes from 100: " + primes(100, 5));
```

The primes() method creates a Stream of an infinite collection of primes, starting at the given input. To get a particular number of elements from the collection we call the limit() method. Then we convert the returned collection of elements into a list and print it. This call to collect() triggers the evaluation of the sequence. The method limit() is also an intermediate operation that lazily notes the number of elements needed for later evaluation! Let's look at this code's output.

```
10 primes from 1: [2, 3, 5, 7, 11, 13, 17, 19, 23, 29]
5 primes from 100: [101, 103, 107, 109, 113]
```

The code produced two series of primes, one starting at 1 and the other starting at 100. These were extracted from the infinite series we created so succinctly within the primes() method, thanks to the laziness of Streams and the power of lambda expressions/method references.

We saw how lambda expressions and the Stream implementations work in tandem to make the execution quite efficient. While lambda expressions and method references make code elegant, expressive, and concise, the real performance gains in Java 8 applications will come from Streams. Lambda expressions are the gateway drug to Java 8, but Streams are the real addiction —be ready to get hooked on them as you develop Java 8 applications.

We got quite a lot done within just a few lines of code; it's perfectly fine to take a few minutes to admire the power of lambda expressions, functional interfaces, and the efficiency of Streams. In the next chapter, we're ready to take the use of lambda expressions up another notch to make recursions more efficient.

Recap

Efficiency got a boost in Java 8; we can be lazy and postpone execution of code until we need it. We can delay initialization of heavyweight resources and easily implement the virtual proxy pattern. Likewise, we can delay evaluation of method arguments to make the calls more efficient. The real heroes of the improved JDK are the Stream interface and the related classes. We can exploit their lazy behaviors to create infinite collections with just a few lines of code. That means highly expressive, concise code to perform complex operations that we couldn't even imagine in Java before.

In the next chapter we'll look at the roles lambda expressions play in optimizing recursions.

Divide each difficulty into as many parts as is feasible and necessary to resolve it.

> ➤ *René Descartes*

CHAPTER 7

Optimizing Recursions

Recursion is a powerful and charming way to solve problems. It's highly expressive—using recursion we can provide a solution to a problem by applying the same solution to its subproblems, an approach known as *divide and conquer*. Various applications employ recursion, such as for finding the shortest distances on a map, computing minimum cost or maximum profit, or reducing waste.

Most languages in use today support recursion. Unfortunately, problems that truly benefit from recursion tend to be fairly large and a simple implementation will quickly result in a stack overflow. In this chapter we'll look at the tail-call optimization (TCO) technique to make recursions feasible for large inputs. Then we'll look into problems that can be expressed using highly recursive overlapping solutions and examine how to make them blazingly fast using the memoization technique.

Using Tail-Call Optimization

The biggest hurdle to using recursion is the risk of stack overflow for problems with large inputs. The brilliant TCO technique can remove that concern. A tail call is a recursive call in which the last operation performed is a call to itself. This is different from a regular recursion, where the function, in addition to making a call to itself, often performs further computations on the result of the recursive call(s). TCO lets us convert regular recursive calls into tail calls to make recursions practical for large inputs.

Java does not directly support TCO at the compiler level, but we can use lambda expressions to implement it in a few lines of code. With this solution, sometimes called *trampoline calls*, we can enjoy the power of recursion without the concern of blowing up the stack.

We'll implement TCO using a very simple and common example, computing a number's factorial.

Starting with an Unoptimized Recursion

Let's start with a piece of code for computing a factorial using a simple unoptimized recursion.

recur/fpij/Factorial.java

```
Line 1  public class Factorial {
     2    public static int factorialRec(final int number) {
     3      if(number == 1)
     4        return number;
     5      else
     6        return number * factorialRec(number - 1);
     7    }
     8  }
```

The recursion terminates when we reach down to the value of 1. For higher values, we recursively call the number times the *factorial* of number minus 1. Let's try out this method using the number 5.

recur/fpij/Factorial.java

```
System.out.println(factorialRec(5));
```

Here's the output for the factorial value.

```
120
```

That seems to work, but let's try it again, this time with a larger input value.

recur/fpij/Factorial.java

```
try {
  System.out.println(factorialRec(20000));
} catch(StackOverflowError ex) {
  System.out.println(ex);
}
```

We coded that call defensively; let's look at the output to see how it turned out.

```
java.lang.StackOverflowError
```

The recursion didn't handle the large input size. It went down with a bang. This is a showstopper in adopting this powerful and expressive technique.

The problem isn't the recursion itself. It's caused by holding the partial result of computations while waiting for the recursion to complete. Let's take a closer look at line 6 in the factorialRec() method. The last operation we perform on that line is multiplication (*). While we hold on to the given number, we wait for the result of the next call to factorialRec() to return. As a consequence we climb the call stack for each call, and the execution of code will eventually blow up if the input size keeps growing. We need a way to be recursive without holding on to the stack.

In *Structure and Interpretation of Computer Programs [AS96]*, Abelson and Sussman discuss the TCO technique, where they convert a recursion into a pure iteration under the hood. Ideally we would like to rely on the compiler to provide such optimization, but since it doesn't, we can use lambda expressions to do this manually, as we'll see next.

Turning to Tail Recursion

Before we can use the TCO technique, we have to redesign our code so it doesn't build up the stack. Instead of waiting to perform the multiplication on line 6 in the factorialRec() method, we can compute the partial product with what we have so far, and pass that on as an extra parameter to the subsequent call. This will remove the need to perform any arithmetic when we return from the recursive call. That's a good first step, but it's not adequate. In addition, we have to step down from the current level of the stack before we recursively call the method. In other words, we need to turn an eager call to factorialRec() into a *lazy* call. We'll use a TailCall functional interface and a companion TailCalls class for this purpose. We'll soon design these two, but let's pretend for now that they already exist.

First let's add static imports to the methods of the TailCalls class.

recur/fpij/Factorial.java
```
import static fpij.TailCalls.done;
import static fpij.TailCalls.call;
```

We'll use these two methods in the new recursive version to compute a factorial, the factorialTailRec() method.

recur/fpij/Factorial.java
```
public static TailCall<Integer> factorialTailRec(
  final int factorial, final int number) {
  if (number == 1)
    return done(factorial);
  else
    return call(() -> factorialTailRec(factorial * number, number - 1));
}
```

This version to compute the factorial is tail recursive; that is, the last operation is a (delayed/lazy) call to itself, and there's no further computation to carry out on the result upon return. Furthermore, rather than calling the method factorialTailRec() eagerly, we wrapped it into a lambda expression for lazy/later execution.

Creating the TailCall Functional Interface

When we call the factorialTailRec() method, it returns immediately with an instance of TailCall. The key idea here is that if we call the done() method, we signal the recursion's termination. On the other hand, if we were to go through the call() method, we would be asking for the recursion to continue, but only after we step down from the current stack level. To fully understand how this works, we have to look inside these methods, so let's drill down into the TailCall interface and the TailCalls companion class. We'll start with the interface.

recur/fpij/TailCall.java

```
@FunctionalInterface
public interface TailCall<T> {

  TailCall<T> apply();

  default boolean isComplete() { return false; }

  default T result() { throw new Error("not implemented"); }

  default T invoke() {
    return Stream.iterate(this, TailCall::apply)
                 .filter(TailCall::isComplete)
                 .findFirst()
                 .get()
                 .result();
  }
}
```

We have four methods in this interface, one abstract and the remaining default. The isComplete() method simply returns a false value. The default implementation of the result() method blows up if called—we would never call this method as long as the recursion is in progress; an alternate implementation of the TailCall interface will take care of the situation when the recursion does terminate.

Critical work is done in the short code within the invoke() method. This method collaborates with the apply() method, which will return the next TailCall instance waiting for execution. The invoke() method has two responsibilities: One, it has to repeatedly iterate through the pending TailCall recursions until it reaches the end of the recursion. Two, upon reaching the end, it has to return the final result (available in the result() method of the terminal TailCall instance).

The invoke() method is short, but there's a lot going on here, so let's slow down and dig into it.

We have no clue how many recursions will be evaluated; it's not infinite, but we can treat it as a series of unknown length. Once we get our heads around treating this as a series of TailCall objects, we can easily use lazy iteration over a Stream of pending TailCall instances. The technique we used in *Creating Infinite, Lazy Collections*, on page 115, will help us here to lazily produce the next pending TailCall instance. Let's take a closer look at how.

To create a lazy list of pending TailCall instances, we use the Stream interface's iterate() static method. This method takes an initial seed value and a generator. We use the current TailCall instance, this, as the seed. The generator, a UnaryOperator, takes in the current element and produces the next element. For the generator to return the next pending TailCall instance it can use the apply() method of the current TailCall. We use the method reference TailCall::apply for this purpose to create the generator.

In short, we've designed the invoke() method so that the iteration will start at the seed, the first instance of TailCall, and iterate through subsequent instances of TailCall produced by the generator until it finds an instance of TailCall that signals the termination of recursion.

Creating the TailCalls Convenience Class

The iteration continues until the isComplete() method reports a completion. But the default() implementation of this method in the TailCall interface always returns a false value. This is where the companion TailCalls class comes in. It provides two different implementations of the TailCall functional interface: one in the call() method and the other in the done() method.

```
recur/fpij/TailCalls.java
public class TailCalls {
  public static <T> TailCall<T> call(final TailCall<T> nextCall) {
    return nextCall;
  }
  public static <T> TailCall<T> done(final T value) {
    return new TailCall<T>() {
      @Override public boolean isComplete() { return true; }
      @Override public T result() { return value; }
      @Override public TailCall<T> apply() {
        throw new Error("not implemented");
      }
    };
  }
}
```

In this class we implement two static methods, call() and done(). The call() method simply receives a TailCall instance and passes it along. It's a convenience method so the recursive calls (such as factorialTailRec()) can nicely end with a symmetric call to either done or call.

In the done() method we return a specialized version of TailCall to indicate the recursion's termination. In this method, we wrap the received value into the specialized instance's *overridden* result() method. The specialized version's isComplete() will report the end of the recursion by returning a true value. Finally, the apply() method throws an exception because this method will never be called on this terminal implementation of TailCall, which signals the end of the recursion.

We can see in this design how the TailCall returned through call() continues recursion, and the one returned from done() terminates it. Also, the recursive calls are all evaluated lazily in a loop in the invoke() default method, thus never increasing the stack level like a simple recursion would.

We designed TailCall and TailCalls for use with factorialTailRec(), but they're reusable for any tail-recursive function.

Using the Tail-Recursive Function

We saw a tail-recursive function factorialTailRec(), a functional interface TailCall, and a convenience class TailCalls. Let's walk through a scenario to understand how all these work together.

Let's start with a call to the factorialTailRec() to compute the factorial of 2, like so:

```
factorialTailRec(1, 2).invoke();
```

The first argument, 1, is the initial value for the factorial; the second argument, 2, is the value for which we'd like to find the factorial. The call to factorialTailRec() will check if the given number is equal to 1 and, since it's not, will use the call() method and pass a lambda expression that synthesizes an instance of TailCall.

This synthesized instance will lazily call the factorialTailRec() with two arguments, 2 and 1, respectively. Back outside the call to the factorialTailRec() method, the call to the invoke() method will create a lazy collection with this first instance of TailCall as the seed and explore the collection until a terminating instance of TailCall is received. When the apply method of the seed TailCall is called, it will result in a call to the factorialTailRec() with the two arguments we mentioned previously. This second call to factorialTailRec() will result in a call to the done() method.

The call to done() will return a terminating specialized instance of TailCall, signaling the recursion's termination. The invoke() method now will return the final result of the computation, 2 in this case.

The TCO of the factorial recursion is complete. Let's take the factorialTailRec() method for a spin. We'll call it with a small value for the input parameter first.

recur/fpij/Factorial.java
```
System.out.println(factorialTailRec(1, 5).invoke());
```

We seed the factorialTailRec() with an initial factorial value, 1 and the number. The result of this call is a TailCall instance and we call the invoke() method on it. That call's result should be the same as the unoptimized recursion version we saw earlier.

```
120
```

Let's run this version with the large input value.

recur/fpij/Factorial.java
```
System.out.println(factorialTailRec(1, 20000).invoke());
```

The previous version ran into a stack overflow. Let's check this version's fate.

```
0
```

The operation succeeded, but the patient died.

Our efforts paid off. We averted blowing up the stack, but the result was 0 due to arithmetic overflow; the factorial result is a very large number. We'll soon fix that—we need to use BigInteger instead of int. Before we address that let's revisit the solution. We have some cleaning up to do.

Cleaning Up the Recursion

The implementation of the factorialTailRec() is alluringly simple. It has one downside, though: we polluted the method's interface. Rather than passing a nice and simple input number, now we have to pass two arguments. We rely on the callers to supply 1 for the first parameter; an argument like 0 would derail the result. Furthermore, we have to call invoke() on the result of the call to factorialTailRec()—not pleasant. We can easily fix these issues by introducing one more level of indirection.

We can turn factorialTailRec() into a private method and introduce a public method that calls it.

recur/fpij/Factorial.java
```java
public static int factorial(final int number) {
  return factorialTailRec(1, number).invoke();
}
```

This method brings back the simple interface and encapsulates the details of tail recursion. It deals with the extra parameter and takes care of calling the necessary invoke() method in the end. Let's use this modified version.

recur/fpij/Factorial.java
```
System.out.println(factorial(5));
System.out.println(factorial(20000));
```

We ran the latest version with a small value and the preposterously large value; let's check out the output.

```
120
0
```

The result was good for the small value, but the large value requires a fix. Let's attend to that as the last step.

Fixing the Arithmetic Overflow

The factorial code was nice and sweet with the int primitive type. To avert the arithmetic overflow, however, we have to switch to BigInteger. Sadly, we'll lose the fluency of simple arithmetic operators like * and - and have to use methods on BigInteger to perform these. We will reduce clutter in the code by creating small functions for these operations in a BigFactorial class.

recur/fpij/BigFactorial.java
```
public class BigFactorial {
  public static BigInteger decrement(final BigInteger number) {
    return number.subtract(BigInteger.ONE);
  }

  public static BigInteger multiply(
    final BigInteger first, final BigInteger second) {
    return first.multiply(second);
  }

  final static BigInteger ONE = BigInteger.ONE;
  final static BigInteger FIVE = new BigInteger("5");
  final static BigInteger TWENTYK = new BigInteger("20000");

  //...
}
```

We wrote some convenience methods and fields to work with BigInteger. Now let's look at the important parts, the encapsulated tail-recursive function and the fluent wrapper around it.

recur/fpij/BigFactorial.java
```
private static TailCall<BigInteger> factorialTailRec(
  final BigInteger factorial, final BigInteger number) {
```

```
    if(number.equals(BigInteger.ONE))
      return done(factorial);
    else
      return call(() ->
        factorialTailRec(multiply(factorial, number), decrement(number)));
}

public static BigInteger factorial(final BigInteger number) {
  return factorialTailRec(BigInteger.ONE, number).invoke();
}
```

Where we used int in the earlier version, we used BigInteger in this version. The rest of the code is pretty much the same, using the TailCall interface, the TailCalls class, and the TCO technique.

Let's call this modified version of factorial().

recur/fpij/BigFactorial.java
```
public static void main(final String[] args) {
  System.out.println(factorial(FIVE));
  System.out.println(String.format("%.10s...", factorial(TWENTYK)));
}
```

Now that we used BigInteger, the operation should go well. Let's visit the patient in recovery.

```
120
1819206320...
```

We see the correct value of the factorial for the number 5, and the trimmed output value for the large input.

With only a few lines of code we turned an unoptimized recursion into a tail recursion and averted stack overflow, thanks to lambda expressions, functional interfaces, and infinite Streams. With this technique on hand we can boldly implement recursive solutions, with a minor redesign to turn them into tail calls.

The approach we used here made recursions feasible for large input. Next we'll see how to make them practical from a performance point of view.

Speeding Up with Memoization

There's a technique to turn excessively recursive problems into incredibly fast execution. We'll explore the problem here and use lambda expressions to implement a solution.

An Optimization Problem

We can see optimization problems in various domains, such as economics, finance, and resource allocation, where an optimal solution is selected from several feasible ones. For example, we may have to find the maximum profit from sales of assets or the shortest route between locations. In an algorithmic technique called *dynamic programming* we apply recursion extensively to solve a problem. This takes recursion to the next level; the solution to a problem overlaps with solutions to subproblems.

If we naively implement such recursion, we'd end up with computations that take exponentially increasing amounts of time to run for increasing input sizes. This is where *memoization* comes in. In this technique we look up solutions if they already exist, and perform and store computations just once. The redundancy that exists in repeatedly asking for the overlapping solutions does not translate into recomputations, but instead turns into a quick lookup for the results. This technique transforms the exponential time complexity to mere linear time. Let's implement this using an example: the rod-cutting problem.[1]

We'll employ a solution for a company that buys rods at wholesale and sells them at retail. They figured that by cutting the rods into different sizes, they could maximize profits. The price that the company can charge for different lengths of rod changes often, so the company wants us to write a program to reveal what the maximum profit would be for a given size of rod. Let's find a simple solution, and then improve on it.

We'll start with a class that stores the prices for different lengths of rod.

recur/fpij/RodCutterBasic.java
```java
public class RodCutterBasic {
  final List<Integer> prices;
  public RodCutterBasic(final List<Integer> pricesForLength) {
    prices = pricesForLength;
  }

  //...
```

Let's work with some sample prices for different lengths, starting with 1 inch.

recur/fpij/RodCutterBasic.java
```java
final List<Integer> priceValues =
  Arrays.asList(2, 1, 1, 2, 2, 2, 1, 8, 9, 15);

final RodCutterBasic rodCutter = new RodCutterBasic(priceValues);
```

---

1.   http://en.wikipedia.org/wiki/Cutting_stock_problem

Plain-Vanilla Recursion

We can solve the problem using a simple recursion. If we're given a 5" rod, we can look up the price for that length. In this example, that would get us $2. We can do better than that—after all, a 4" rod also would fetch $2, so we could cut the rod into two pieces—4" and 1"—to increase profit. Continuing with this approach, we find that the profit for an arbitrary length n is the maximum of the profits from each of the possible 2^{n-1} cuts of that length. That is, max(no cut, cut(1, n - 1), cut(2, n - 2), ...), for a given length n. The next figure is an example of profits from all possible cuts for a 5" rod.

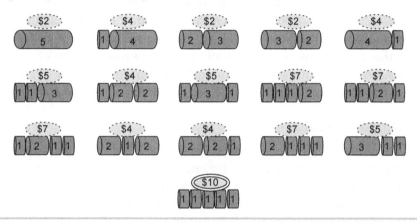

Figure 9—Calculating the maximum profit for a 5" rod by exploring 16 possible cuts

To compute the profit for 5" we need to compute the profit for 4", 3", 2", and 1". Likewise, to compute the profit for 4" we need to compute the profit for the smaller sizes. The solution nicely introduces overlapping recursion; we'll implement this without any optimization first, and then improve on it.

Let's implement the logic for maximum profit.

```
recur/fpij/RodCutterBasic.java
public int maxProfit(final int length) {
  int profit = (length <= prices.size()) ? prices.get(length - 1) : 0;
  for(int i = 1; i < length; i++) {
    int priceWhenCut = maxProfit(i) + maxProfit(length - i);
    if(profit < priceWhenCut) profit = priceWhenCut;
  }

  return profit;
}
```

In the maxProfit() method we look up the price for a particular length. Then we recursively find the profit for lengths that add up to the given length, and pick the maximum from them. The implementation turns out to be quite simple. Let's try it for a few lengths.

```
recur/fpij/RodCutterBasic.java
System.out.println(rodCutter.maxProfit(5));
System.out.println(rodCutter.maxProfit(22));
```

Let's look at the output for the different lengths.

```
10
44
```

The output seems reasonable, but the computation for this would take a long time, like 45 seconds, depending on system speed. If we increase the length slightly from 22, the program will slow a lot, into minutes and hours. That's because the time complexity of this computation is exponential—$O(2^{n-1})$—we're performing the computations redundantly for various lengths. We need to memoize the results to speed up execution—a lot.

Memoizing the Results

Memoization is a simple yet smart technique to make recursive overlapping computations really fast. Using this technique, as the program runs we make calculations only if they have not been made already. Each time a new calculation happens, we cache the results and reuse those for subsequent calls for the same input. This technique is useful only if the computations are expected to return the same result each time for a given input. Our rod-cutting problem fits that requirement: the profit is the same for a given length and a given set of prices, no matter how many times we ask. Let's memoize the result of the profit calculation.

When seeking the profit for a sublength, we can skip the computation if the profit for that length has been already been computed. This will speed up the program, as the redundant calls to find the profit will turn into a quick lookup of a hashmap. Sounds good, but it would be nice to have reusable code for that. Let's create a reusable class; we'll call it the Memoizer. It does not yet exist, but we'll pretend it does and write the code to use it. Let's refactor the maxProfit() method to use a static method, callMemoized(), of the Memoizer class.

```java
public int maxProfit(final int rodLength) {
  BiFunction<Function<Integer, Integer>, Integer, Integer> compute =
    (func, length) -> {
      int profit = (length <= prices.size()) ? prices.get(length - 1) : 0;
      for(int i = 1; i < length; i++) {
        int priceWhenCut = func.apply(i) + func.apply(length - i);
        if(profit < priceWhenCut) profit = priceWhenCut;
      }
```

```
      return profit;
    };
  return callMemoized(compute, rodLength);
}
```

Let's look at the crux of the design before we dig into the code. We create a function and memoize it. The memoized version will look up values before making a call to the actual implementation. Let's figure out how we achieve this.

In the maxProfit() method we call the (yet-to-be-implemented) Memoizer's callMemoized() method. This function takes a lambda expression as an argument. This lambda expression has two parameters, a reference to the memoized version of the function and the incoming parameter. Within the lambda expression, we perform our task, and when it's time to recurse we route the call to the memoized reference. This will return quickly if the value has been cached or memoized. Otherwise, it will recursively route the call to this lambda expression to compute for that length.

The missing piece of the puzzle is the memoized reference we receive from the callMemoized() method, so let's look at the Memoizer class's implementation.

recur/fpij/Memoizer.java
```
public class Memoizer {
  public static <T, R> R callMemoized(
    final BiFunction<Function<T,R>, T, R> function, final T input) {
    Function<T, R> memoized = new Function<T, R>() {
      private final Map<T, R> store = new HashMap<>();
      public R apply(final T input) {
        return store.computeIfAbsent(input, key -> function.apply(this, key));
      }
    };
    return memoized.apply(input);
  }
}
```

The Memoizer has just one short function. In callMemoized() we create an implementation of Function in which we check to see if the solution for a given input is already present. We use the newly added computeIfAbsent() method of Map. If a value is present for the given input, we return it; otherwise we forward the call to the intended function and send a reference to the memoized function so the intended function can swing back here for subsequent computations.

This version of the maxProfit() method nicely encapsulates the details of memoization. The call to this method looks the same as the previous version:

```
System.out.println(rodCutter.maxProfit(5));
System.out.println(rodCutter.maxProfit(22));
```

Let's run the memoized version and ensure the profit reported is the same as in the previous version.

```
10
44
```

The profit is consistent between the versions, but the execution speeds are a world apart. The memoized version took less than 0.15 seconds, compared to around 45 seconds for the previous version. With this memoized version, we can easily bump up our rod lengths to large values and still take only a fraction of a second to get the results. For example, a length of 500" makes no dent on the execution time; it's blazingly fast.

In this chapter we used lambda expressions and infinite Streams to implement TCO and memoization. The examples show us how the new features in Java 8 can come together to create powerful solutions. You can use similar techniques to create nifty solutions to your own complex problems.

Recap

Recursions are a valuable tool in programming, but a simple implementation of recursion is often not useful for practical problems. Functional interfaces, lambda expression, and infinite Streams can help us design tail-call optimization to make recursions feasible in such cases. Furthermore, we can combine recursions and memoization to make execution of overlapping recursions really fast.

In the next chapter we'll explore a practical example that employs lambda expressions and then we'll parallelize it with little effort.

Programs must be written for people to read, and only incidentally for machines to execute.[1]

> ▷ *Hal Abelson and Jerry Sussman*

CHAPTER 8

Composing with Lambda Expressions

With Java 8 we have two powerful tools: the object-oriented approach and the functional style. They are not mutually exclusive; they can work together for the greater good.

In OOP we often mutate state. If we combine OOP with the functional style, we can instead transform objects by passing lightweight objects through a series of cohesive functions. This can help us create code that's easier to extend—to produce a different result we simply alter the way the functions are composed. We can use the functions, in addition to the objects, as components to program with.

In this chapter we look into function composition. Then we use that to create a practical working example of the popular MapReduce pattern, where we scatter independent calculations, and gather the results to create the solution. As a final step, we parallelize those calculations almost effortlessly, thanks to the ubiquitous JDK library.

Using Function Composition

The OOP paradigm helps us realize abstraction, encapsulation, and polymorphism; inheritance is the weakest link in the paradigm. When programming in the functional style we compose higher-order functions, and as much as possible, promote immutability and functions. We can leverage our experience with OOP, and at the same time use the elegant functional style that is new in Java.

Let's get a feel for object transformation. Suppose we need change, and we ask a friend to break a $10 bill. We don't expect our buddy to tear up the bill and return the pieces. Instead, we'd like the bill to disappear into our friend's

---

1. Structure and Interpretation of Computer Programs [AS96] (http://mitpress.mit.edu/sicp)

pocket and some smaller bills to appear. Mixing OOP and functional style is like that; we send lightweight objects to functions and expect other objects to emerge.

In this combined approach, to achieve a task we chain a series of appropriate functions. As objects pass through the functions in the series, they transform into new objects to produce the desired result. We can see the difference between a pure OOP and a mixed OOP-functional style in the following figure. In pure OOP, at least the way it's used in Java, over time an object's state goes through transitions. In the combined approach, we see lightweight objects transform into other objects rather than transition state.

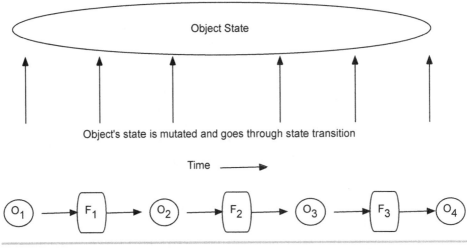

Figure 10—Pure OOP vs. hybrid OOP-functional style

Let's work with an example to get a better feel for this. We'll start with a list of ticker symbols and, from it, create a sorted list, with each item corresponding stock valued over \$100. In the habitual approach we'd walk through the list using an external iterator and update a mutable collection. Instead we'll transform objects. We'll filter the tickers list into a list of tickers priced over \$100, then sort the list, and finally report.

We need a sample list of ticker symbols, so let's start with that.

```
applying/fpij/Tickers.java
public class Tickers {
  public static final List<String> symbols = Arrays.asList(
    "AMD", "HPQ", "IBM", "TXN", "VMW", "XRX", "AAPL", "ADBE",
    "AMZN", "CRAY", "CSCO", "SNE", "GOOG", "INTC", "INTU",
    "MSFT", "ORCL", "TIBX", "VRSN", "YHOO");
}
```

We have some twenty symbols in this sample list. We need to determine the price for each stock. We saw the code to fetch the latest price from Yahoo! in *Integrating with the Web Service*, on page 71; we can reuse that here. Let's revisit that code to refresh our memory.

designing/fpij/YahooFinance.java

```
public class YahooFinance {
  public static BigDecimal getPrice(final String ticker) {
    try {
      final URL url =
        new URL("http://ichart.finance.yahoo.com/table.csv?s=" + ticker);

      final BufferedReader reader =
        new BufferedReader(new InputStreamReader(url.openStream()));
      final String data = reader.lines().skip(1).findFirst().get();
      final String[] dataItems = data.split(",");
      return new BigDecimal(dataItems[dataItems.length - 1]);
    } catch(Exception ex) {
      throw new RuntimeException(ex);
    }
  }
}
```

The getPrice() method will return the latest price for a given stock. Since we're looking for only stocks valued over $100, we can use Stream's filter() method to trim down the list. Once we get the short list, we can sort it easily using Stream's sorted() method. Finally we can concatenate the symbols to print. These are all operations we've seen before, coming together here to help with this task. Let's look at the code.

applying/fpij/Stocks100.java

```
final BigDecimal HUNDRED = new BigDecimal("100");
System.out.println("Stocks priced over $100 are " +
  Tickers.symbols
         .stream()
         .filter(
           symbol -> YahooFinance.getPrice(symbol).compareTo(HUNDRED) > 0)
         .sorted()
         .collect(joining(", ")));
```

The series of operations flows nicely in a chain. The operations are associative; the stream of ticker symbols is filtered, sorted, and concatenated. As we move through the composed functions, the original list of symbols is left unmodified, but we transform from that into a filtered stream of symbols, then into a stream of sorted symbols. We finally join the symbols in this last stream for printing. If instead of sorting we want to pick a particular symbol, let's say the first, we only have to slightly alter the chain; we can reuse most of the functions. Let's visit the stock market to see which stocks in the list are valued at over $100.

```
Stocks priced over $100 are AAPL, AMZN, GOOG, IBM
```

The ability to compose functions into a chain of operations is powerful and has quite a few benefits. It makes the code easier to understand. The lack of mutability reduces the chance of errors and makes it easier to parallelize the code. We can alter a few links in the chain and easily alter the behavior along the way. We'll see these benefits come to life in the next examples.

Using MapReduce

In the *MapReduce* pattern we express two sets of operations, one to perform on each element in a collection and one to combine these results to arrive at a final result. This pattern is gaining attention due to its simplicity and power to exploit multicore processors.

The JVM is all geared up to utilize multicore processors. To fully benefit from the true power of the JVM and multicore processors, however, we have to change the way we code. In this section we'll explore the MapReduce pattern with an example, and in the next section we'll build on that example to parallelize it.

Let's continue with the example we've been using. Given a list of ticker symbols, let's pick the highest-priced stock whose value is less than $500. Let's work this example first using the imperative style and quickly evolve it to the functional style. This will help us see the difference in style and how to transition from the familiar style to functional style in a more of a real-world scenario.

Preparing the Computations

To start we need some utility functions to get the prices, compare them, and so forth. Let's cover those first.

To help easily work with the stock names and prices, let's create a class with immutable fields.

```
applying/fpij/StockInfo.java
public class StockInfo {
  public final String ticker;
  public final BigDecimal price;
  public StockInfo(final String symbol, final BigDecimal thePrice) {
    ticker = symbol;
    price = thePrice;
  }
```

```
  public String toString() {
    return String.format("ticker: %s price: %g", ticker, price);
  }
}
```

The StockInfo is simply a value object; it holds a ticker symbol and its price. Given a ticker, we need a function to create an instance of StockInfo with the price information filled in. We'll reuse YahooFinance's getPrice() method in the implementation of this function.

applying/fpij/StockUtil.java
```
public class StockUtil {
  public static StockInfo getPrice(final String ticker) {
    return new StockInfo(ticker, YahooFinance.getPrice(ticker));
  }
  //...
}
```

The getPrice() method is simply a wrapper, a convenience method. We need a method to tell us if the price is less than the desired amount, so let's create that.

applying/fpij/StockUtil.java
```
public static Predicate<StockInfo> isPriceLessThan(final int price) {
  return
    stockInfo -> stockInfo.price.compareTo(BigDecimal.valueOf(price)) < 0;
}
```

This is a higher-order method. It takes a price value and returns a Predicate that can be evaluated later to check if a given instance of StockInfo is less than the price value cached in the lambda expression. The last convenience method will help us pick the highest-priced stock from a pair.

applying/fpij/StockUtil.java
```
public static StockInfo pickHigh(
  final StockInfo stock1, final StockInfo stock2) {
  return stock1.price.compareTo(stock2.price) > 0 ? stock1 : stock2;
}
```

pickHigh() simply returns an instance of StockInfo with the highest price from the pair of instances given to it. We've created the functions we need and we're all set to put them to work. Let's create the imperative version of the code to get the highest-priced stock in the range.

Moving from the Imperative Style…

We're accustomed to imperative programming, but as we'll see here, it can be a lot of work.

```
applying/fpij/PickStockImperative.java
final List<StockInfo> stocks = new ArrayList<>();
for(String symbol : Tickers.symbols) {
  stocks.add(StockUtil.getPrice(symbol));
}

final List<StockInfo> stocksPricedUnder500 = new ArrayList<>();
final Predicate<StockInfo> isPriceLessThan500 = StockUtil.isPriceLessThan(500);
for(StockInfo stock : stocks) {
  if(isPriceLessThan500.test(stock))
    stocksPricedUnder500.add(stock);
}

StockInfo highPriced = new StockInfo("", BigDecimal.ZERO);
for(StockInfo stock : stocksPricedUnder500) {
  highPriced = StockUtil.pickHigh(highPriced, stock);
}

System.out.println("High priced under $500 is " + highPriced);
```

We created three loops. In the first one we made a list of StockInfo filled with
the price for each of the symbols. In the second loop we made a trimmed-
down list of stock info, restricting it to stocks under $500. In the final loop
we picked the highest-priced stock among the candidates. Let's see which
stock gets picked.

```
High priced under $500 is ticker: AMZN price: 376.640
```

In that code, we see three distinct steps, from symbols to stocks, then to
selected stocks, and finally to the highest priced among the selected stocks.
We can combine the operations all into one loop if we like. Here's the clubbed
imperative version:

```
applying/fpij/PickStockImperativeClubbed.java
StockInfo highPriced = new StockInfo("", BigDecimal.ZERO);
final Predicate<StockInfo> isPriceLessThan500 = StockUtil.isPriceLessThan(500);

for(String symbol : Tickers.symbols) {
  StockInfo stockInfo = StockUtil.getPrice(symbol);

  if(isPriceLessThan500.test(stockInfo))
    highPriced = StockUtil.pickHigh(highPriced, stockInfo);
}
System.out.println("High priced under $500 is " + highPriced);
```

With this step, we gained some and lost some. We reduced the code and
removed a few loops; less code is better. But we're still being imperative,
mutating variables. Furthermore, if we want to change the logic—say we want
to pick the highest-priced stock under $1,000—we have to modify this code.

No part of it is reusable. Going back to our three-step version of the code, we could modularize each part into a function for reuse. Rather than combining the steps, if we keep them as distinct steps we can convert them easily from the imperative style to the functional style, as we'll see next.

...To the Functional Style

We used three different loops in the imperative version, but the JDK provides specialized functional-style methods for each of those steps. We can easily use those convenience methods and we won't have to manually create any internal iterators to program the logic in the functional style. Let's refactor the code into the functional style; this version is declarative, preserves immutability, is concise, and uses function composition.

```
applying/fpij/PickStockFunctional.java
public static void findHighPriced(final Stream<String> symbols) {
  final StockInfo highPriced =
    symbols.map(StockUtil::getPrice)
           .filter(StockUtil.isPriceLessThan(500))
           .reduce(StockUtil::pickHigh)
           .get();

  System.out.println("High priced under $500 is " + highPriced);
}
```

In the method findHighPriced(), we employ method chaining and transform objects. We start with a Stream of symbols and flow into streams of stocks. We first map the symbols into stocks filled with prices. Following the map operation, we trim down the list and reduce it to a single value. The reduce() function gives us some extra control, but if we simply want to pick the highest value, we could instead use the max() method on the Stream.

This version has about half as many lines as the multistep imperative version. It has about the same number of lines as the clubbed imperative version. In addition to being concise, this code has a few benefits. The biggest gain is that the ability to parallelize this code comes for free, as we'll see in the next section. We derive this benefit by using function composition and higher-order functions, and avoiding mutability. This version of code is easier to understand —the symbols are mapped into StockInfo, then filtered to the desired range, and finally reduced to a single object containing the highest value and the corresponding ticker symbol.

We need to convert from the List of symbols, in Tickers, to a Stream of symbols before we call the findHighPriced() method.

```
findHighPriced(Tickers.symbols.stream());
```

Let's run the code and ensure the result is the same as the imperative version.

```
High priced under $500 is ticker: AMZN price: 376.640
```

The code is quite concise and this version picked the same stock, at the same price, as the previous version.

Let's take a minute to visualize, in the following figure, the operations we performed in this example.

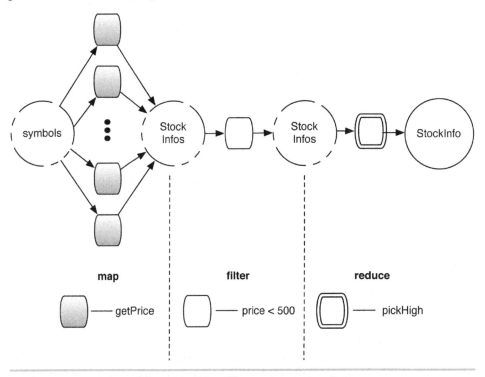

Figure 11—Map-filter-reduce operation

In the figure we see the *map* operation applies the function to fetch the stock prices on each element in the symbols collection. This gives us the stream of StockInfo instances, which we then *filter* to select stocks, and finally we apply the *reduce* operation to distill this to one StockInfo object. The layout of the operations in the figure shows the potential for parallelization. We'll dig into that next.

Taking a Leap to Parallelize

We can easily parallelize the previous example to speed up the execution.

Let's take a closer look at the code before we make any changes. We send the tickers though the map() method, which sequentially invokes the attached function to get the price from Yahoo! Once all the prices arrive, we sequentially trim the list to stocks within the desired price range. In the last step, which is also sequential, we pick the highest priced among them.

Of these three operations, the first is the slowest. It involves a call to the web service, incurs a network delay, and has to perform the operation 20 times—once for each ticker symbol. The remaining operations involve light arithmetic and hardly take any time. Thankfully, in this problem the slowest parts are independent of each other and can be performed all at once.

We don't have to wait for Yahoo! to respond to the price for one ticker symbol before we send out the request for the next. Web services are quite capable of handling multiple requests concurrently, barring any limits imposed by a particular vendor to set free-of-charge or basic service apart from premium services they may sell.

Let's run the previous version once more to see how long it took to pick the highest-priced stock valued under $500. The following output was produced by running the program with the UNIX-based time utility.

```
High priced under $500 is ticker: AMZN price: 376.640

real    0m17.688s
user    0m0.269s
sys     0m0.053s
```

The time it takes to run will vary, depending on the quality of the network connection. On my wireless network it took a little more than 17 seconds for the imperative, sequential version to pick the appropriate stock. Let's parallelize the code and see how that fares.

Making code concurrent is a big topic—where do we start and how do we proceed? We have to distribute the tasks onto multiple threads, then collect the results, then move on to the sequential steps. While we're at it, we must ensure there are no race conditions; we don't want threads to collide with other threads' updates and mess up the data.

There are two concerns here: one is how to do it and the other is how to do it properly. For the first concern, we can seek the help of libraries to manage threads. The responsibility for doing it right falls on us. Race conditions arise largely from shared mutability. If multiple threads try to update an object or a variable at the same time, we have to ensure thread safety. This concern disappears if we follow good functional style and honor immutability.

Surprisingly, with the design we created the code is only one step away from running parallel rather than sequentially. We need to switch only one call, from this:

```
findHighPriced(Tickers.symbols.stream());
```

to this:

```
findHighPriced(Tickers.symbols.parallelStream());
```

stream() and parallelStream() have the same return type, but the instances they return are quite different. parallelStream()'s returned instance runs methods like map() and filter() in parallel across multiple threads, managed by a thread pool under the hood. The benefit is that we can easily switch between sequential and concurrent versions, and methods like findHighPriced() can be oblivious to parallelism.

Let's run the parallelized version of the code and look at the time it takes to run. Again, I produced the following output using the time utility.

```
High priced under $500 is ticker: AMZN price: 376.640

real    0m3.022s
user    0m0.266s
sys     0m0.049s
```

The first bit of good news is that this version picked the same stock as the sequential version. After all, there's no point running really fast in the wrong direction. The second bit of good news is the speed of execution. The parallelized version took about 3 seconds on the same wireless network used for the previous version. Again, the network speed has an impact on the execution time we would observe on each run.

When deciding whether to call stream() or parallelStream(), we have to consider a few issues. First, do we really want to run the lambda expressions concurrently? Second, the code should be able to run independently without causing any side effects or race conditions. Third, the correctness of the solution should not depend on the order of execution of the lambda expressions that are scheduled to run concurrently. For example, it would not make sense to parallelize calls to the forEach() method and print results from within the lambda expression we provide. Since the order of execution is not predictable, the order of output may be quite confusing. On the other hand, methods like map() and filter() that can perform computations and forward their results for further processing are good candidates; see the following sidebar.

> **\\// Joe asks:**
> **ᴗᴗ Should We Choose Parallel Streams?**
>
> The library makes it easy to go parallel, but sometimes that's not the right choice. It depends on your data and your computation. Sometimes a parallel computation may be *slower* than its sequential counterpart.
>
> We often look to concurrency to speed up execution. However, there is a cost—execution time—to make things concurrent. We have to evaluate to make sure that the time savings far outweighs the cost of using concurrency.
>
> For small collections, if the tasks per element are fairly short and quick, the sequential execution may beat any concurrent solution. The benefits of concurrency will shine only if the tasks are time consuming and the collection is fairly large.
>
> Even though parallel streams in Java 8 make it pretty easy to make code concurrent, we still have to evaluate based on the problem at hand and the data size to decide if there's an execution-time savings.

The change from sequential to parallel was effortless, but we did quite a number of things to make this possible. First, we avoided mutability and kept the functions pure, with no side effects. We avoided race conditions and thread-safety issues, which is critical for correctness—there's no point being fast and incorrect. We should take extreme care to ensure that lambda expressions passed to stream operations are side effect–free.

Second, the way we composed the functions helped. The decision to run sequentially or in parallel was made upstream, when we transformed the List to a Stream. The rest of the code in the findHighPriced() method didn't change; the two versions share it in common. Going from sequential to parallel was as simple as toggling a switch.

Recap

Lambda expressions help compose functions into a chain of operations, which lets us put problems into an associative series of object transformations. In addition, by preserving immutability and avoiding side effects we can easily parallelize execution of parts of the chain's operations and gain on speed.

In the next chapter we wrap up with a discussion of making good use of the functional style, and address some limitations.

Any intelligent fool can make things bigger, more complex, and
more violent. It takes a touch of genius—and a lot of courage—
to move in the opposite direction.
> *Albert Einstein*

CHAPTER 9

Bringing It All Together

We explored Java 8 lambda expressions throughout this book, using them to iterate over collections, to achieve better lightweight design, and to easily compose and parallelize code. In this final chapter we'll bring it all together. We'll review the practices we have to hone to fully benefit from functional style, then discuss the performance impact of this style and conclude with some recommendations on how we can successfully adopt the functional style.

Essential Practices to Succeed with the Functional Style

The new features in Java 8 do not just change the syntax we type. To benefit fully and create highly concise and lightweight applications, we need to change the designs, the code, and our thinking; it's different from the imperative and object-oriented paradigm we're used to in Java. Let's go over some of the fundamental ways we have to change how we develop applications, and the benefits we'll receive in return.

More Declarative, Less Imperative

We have to raise the level of abstraction. Rather than imperatively focusing on the steps to take, we have to think and express declaratively the bigger goals we want to achieve. For example, instead of commanding the computer to step through each element in a collection, we ask it to filter out the elements we want or to map or transform it into yet another collection. This can help take the "Tell, Don't Ask" principle further and make the code more concise and expressive.[1]

---

1.   http://pragprog.com/articles/tell-dont-ask

For example, let's say we're given a list of stock prices and asked to pick the maximum value. From experience, our first instinct may be to write it imperatively like this:

```
int max = 0;
for(int price : prices) {
  if(max < price) max = price;
}
```

Instead let's think declaratively. We'll tell the program to pick the max rather than ask it to walk through each step:

```
final int max = prices.stream()
                      .reduce(0, Math::max);
```

The benefits go far beyond having fewer lines of code. We have fewer chances to introduce errors—the code we don't write has the fewest bugs. Having fewer lines of understandable code is simpler than many lines of fluffy code.

Imperative code is primitive and involves more mutability. On the other hand, declarative code raises the level of abstraction and reduces the need for mutable variables. This also lowers the chances of errors in code.

Favor Immutability

Mutable variables are in poor taste, and shared mutable variables are pure evil. We often get confused or overlook change to variables. As a result, code with more mutable variables tends to have more errors. Code with shared mutable variables is very hard to parallelize correctly. One way to reduce errors is simply to avoid mutability where possible, and the functional style makes that easier.

Purely functional languages have only values: write-once variables that can't change after initialization. Since Java does not enforce immutability, the onus is on us to favor immutability. When we encounter mutable variables, we can examine the libraries to see if there's a functional-style equivalent that will eliminate them.

Reduce Side Effects

A function with no side effects is not affected by anything outside and does not affect anything outside of its bounds. Functions or methods with side effects are hard to understand, hard to maintain, more error prone, and difficult to parallelize.

If we remove side effects, then as long as the input to a function remains unchanged, the output will always be the same. This makes it easier to understand the code and makes us need fewer test cases to ensure the proper behavior.

Having no side effects is critical for *referential transparency*, which means an invocation or a call to a function can be replaced by its result value without affecting a program's correctness. The functional style greatly favors creating functions with no side effects, and the benefits are far reaching.

The javac compiler and the JVM just-in-time compiler can easily optimize calls to functions with no side effects. Functions that have side effects impose ordering and restrict optimization. On the other hand, calls to functions with no side effects can be moved around and reordered more freely. For example, in the next figure F_1 and F_2 are two independent function calls. The compiler can change the order of their sequential execution or even schedule them to run concurrently on multiple cores, thanks to their referential transparent behavior.

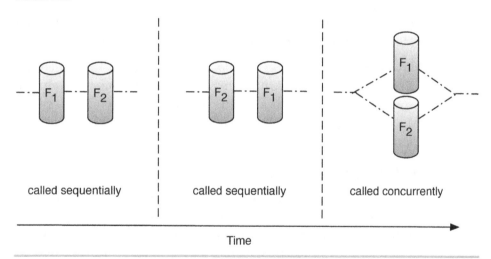

Figure 12—We can easily reorder functions that have no side effects.

When working with lambda expressions, we should ensure that the code is without side effects. Doing so will not only reduce the chance of errors, but also help us easily parallelize the code, as we saw in *Taking a Leap to Parallelize*, on page 143. It's critical to eliminate side effects if we want to use techniques like the tail-call optimization we saw in *Using Tail-Call Optimization*, on page 121.

Prefer Expressions Over Statements

Both expressions and statements are commands we write in programs to instruct the computer to perform some action or do some work. Statements perform actions but don't return anything, whereas expressions perform actions and return a result. When programming with lambda expressions we can reap benefits by leaning toward creating expressions more than statements.

First, since statements don't return anything, they have to cause side effects and mutate memory to fulfill their purpose. Expressions, on the other hand, can be designed to favor referential transparency, giving us the benefits we discussed previously.

The other benefit is that unlike statements, expressions can be composed. This can help us use a very powerful pattern in the functional style of programming—function chaining. We can create a chain of functions so the results of computations flow smoothly from one function into the next. The code begins to read like the problem statement, making it easier to follow.

We saw a benefit of this in ...*To the Functional Style*, on page 141, where we sent a list of stock-ticker symbols through a chain of functions to determine the highest-priced stock and its price. This pattern can also help us create fluent interfaces, as we saw in *Creating Fluent Interfaces Using Lambda Expressions*, on page 80.

Design with Higher-Order Functions

In Java 8, one of the biggest changes we have to make is to design with higher-order functions. We're used to passing objects to methods, but now we also have the ability to pass functions as arguments. This gives us more concise code: anywhere we passed anonymous inner classes to single method interfaces, we can now pass lambda expressions or method references.

For example, to register a simple event handler for a Swing button, we had to jump through hoops before, like in the next example.

```
button.addActionListener(new ActionListener() {
  public void actionPerformed(ActionEvent event) {
    JOptionPane.showMessageDialog(frame, "you clicked!");
  }
});
```

We can trade such clunky code in for more concise code, like this:

```
button.addActionListener(event ->
  JOptionPane.showMessageDialog(frame, "you clicked!"));
```

The ceremony and the clutter are gone, leaving behind just the essence. Not only did we write fewer lines of code here, but we also needed fewer imports in the code. That's because we no longer have to refer to the ActionListener interface by name, and the reference to ActionEvent is optional since we used type inference.

Once we get used to lambda expressions, they will have a lot of impact on our designs. We can design our methods to receive functional interfaces as parameters. This will enable the callers to pass in either lambda expressions or method references as arguments, which will help us take a lightweight approach to separating concerns from methods and classes, like we discussed in Chapter 4, *Designing with Lambda Expressions*, on page 63. The common, familiar design patterns are more approachable when we design with lambda expressions; we need fewer lines of code, classes, and interfaces, and far less ceremony to implement our designs.

Performance Concerns

Java has come a long way and is used in a vast number of enterprise applications where performance is critical. It's reasonable to ask if the new features will affect performance. The answer is yes, but mostly for the better!

Before we dig into that, let's recall Donald Knuth's wise words: "We should forget about small efficiencies, say about 97% of the time: premature optimization is the root of all evil."[2] With that in mind, we should boldly try out the new style where it makes sense. If the performance we get is adequate for the needs of the application, we can move on. Otherwise, we have to critically evaluate the design and profile the code to figure out the real bottlenecks.

The Java 8 specification provides a great amount of flexibility to facilitate compiler optimizations. This, in combination with the relatively new *invoke-dynamic* optimized bytecode instruction, can make the calls using lambda expressions quite fast.[3] Let's look at the performance.

Here's imperative code to count the number of primes in a collection of numbers.

```
long primesCount = 0;
for(long number : numbers) {
  if(isPrime(number)) primesCount += 1;
}
```

---

2. http://c2.com/cgi/wiki?PrematureOptimization
3. See Brian Goetz's JavaOne 2012 presentation "Lambda: A Peek under the Hood"—http://tinyurl.com/abbonw4.

We're using the habitual for loop to invoke a method isPrime() to determine if each number in the collection is prime. If a number is prime, we increment the primesCount mutable variable. Let's measure the time to run this code for a large collection, say 100,000 numbers.

```
0.0250944 seconds
```

That took about 0.02 second, but the code is in the style we want to curtail; let's see if the new style we want to adopt will stand up to this performance. Let's refactor that code to our favorite functional style: code that's declarative, is created in favor of immutability, has no side effects, and is composed of higher-order functions chained together.

```
final long primesCount =
  numbers.stream()
        .filter(number -> isPrime(number))
        .count();
```

We transformed the collection into a Stream and then used the filter() method to pick only primes from the collection. Then we got the size of the filtered collection. In essence we asked the code to filter out just the primes in the collection. Let's see how much time this version takes to run on the same collection as the previous version.

```
0.0253816 seconds
```

From the output we see that the performance using lambda expression is about the same; we did not lose anything, but we have gained quite a bit. It's trivial to parallelize the functional-style version. To parallelize the imperative version, on the other hand, we have to...um...that's a slippery slope we want to avoid.

Let's waste no time. Here's the parallelized functional-style version:

```
final long primesCount =
  numbers.parallelStream()
        .filter(number -> isPrime(number))
        .count();
```

That was hardly any effort. Let's see the gain in speed by running the code.

```
0.00649266 seconds
```

The parallelized version, running on a quad-core processor, took about 0.006 second.

Before we run off to celebrate this glorious performance, let's admit that a large number of performance metrics are contrived and we can't blindly rely on them. If nothing else, this example simply shows that using lambda expressions and the functional style does not have to mean poor performance.

When creating real code for enterprise applications, we have to keep an eye on performance and address concerns where they arise.

Adopting the Functional Style

Picking up new syntax is relatively easy, but changing the way we design and think takes more effort. Programming in the functional style in Java is a paradigm shift, and we've seen examples that show this change is good. Let's discuss some ways in which we can make an easy and successful transition to this exciting new world in Java.

Following a few practices we discussed in *Essential Practices to Succeed with the Functional Style*, on page 147, will help us get better at functional-style coding. Java is now a mixed-paradigm language with support for imperative, object-oriented, and functional programming. We have to judiciously balance them, but the ability to do so comes from experience, trying out designs, and evaluating the trade-offs.

At the beginning of the transition to this paradigm, it's quite natural to continue to think in the most familiar ways. That's fine; we can implement and quickly refactor the code; "Make it work, then make it better (real soon)" is a good mantra to follow. With experience, the need for these refactoring efforts will diminish and more functional-style code will flow more naturally.

To get better at what we do, we have to be willing to change our ways. This means we have to fearlessly try out our ideas and then improve based on feedback from our colleagues. We can benefit a great deal from tactical code reviews, pair-programming sessions, and brown-bag sessions at work. Outside of work, special-interest groups like the local Java user groups are great places for us to expand our knowledge. We can participate in local study groups or help organize one if none exist.

Java 8 and lambda expressions will improve the way we develop software. These powerful features have breathed new life into today's most popular language. It's an exciting time to be a programmer.

Program well, and in style.

Starter Set of Functional Interfaces

JDK 8 has a number of functional interfaces. Here we review the starter set—the interfaces we frequently encounter and need to get familiar with. All the interfaces we see here are part of the java.util.function package.

Consumer<T>

Description	Represents an operation that will accept an input and returns nothing. For this to be useful, it will have to cause side effects.
Abstract method	accept()
default method(s)	andThen()
Popular usage	As a parameter to the forEach() method
Primitive specializations	IntConsumer, LongConsumer, DoubleConsumer, ...

Supplier<T>

Description	A factory that's expected to return either a new instance or a precreated instance
Abstract method	get()
default method(s)	—
Popular usage	To create lazy infinite Streams and as the parameter to the Optional class's orElseGet() method
Primitive specializations	IntSupplier, LongSupplier, DoubleSupplier, ...

Predicate<T>

Description	Useful for checking if an input argument satisfies some condition

Abstract method	test()
default method(s)	and(), negate(), and or()
Popular usage	As a parameter to Stream's methods, like filter() and anyMatch()
Primitive specializations	IntPredicate, LongPredicate, DoublePredicate, ...

Function<T, R>

Description	A transformational interface that represents an operation intended to take in an argument and return an appropriate result
Abstract method	apply()
default method(s)	andThen(), compose()
Popular usage	As a parameter to Stream's map() method
Primitive specializations	IntFunction, LongFunction, DoubleFunction, IntToDoubleFunction, DoubleToIntFunction, ...

Syntax Overview

We've played with the new syntax for functional interfaces, lambda expressions, method references, and constructor references throughout this book. This appendix is a quick reference for syntax, using sample code selected from various parts of the book.

Defining a Functional Interface

```
@FunctionalInterface
public interface TailCall<T> {

  TailCall<T> apply();

  default boolean isComplete() { return false; }
  //...
}
```

A functional interface must have one abstract—unimplemented—method. It may have zero or more default or implemented methods. It may also have static methods.

Creating No-Parameter Lambda Expressions

```
lazyEvaluator(() -> evaluate(1), () -> evaluate(2));
```

The parentheses () around the empty parameters list are required if the lambda expression takes no parameters. The -> separates the parameters from the body of a lambda expression.

Creating a Single-Parameter Lambda Expression

```
friends.forEach((final String name) -> System.out.println(name));
```

The Java compiler can infer the type of lambda expression based on the context. In some situations where the context is not adequate for it to infer or we want better clarity, we can specify the type in front of the parameter names.

Inferring a Lambda Expression's Parameter Type

```
friends.forEach((name) -> System.out.println(name));
```

The Java compiler will try to infer the types for parameters if we don't provide them. Using inferred types is less noisy and requires less effort, but if we specify the type for one parameter, we have to specify it for all parameters in a lambda expression.

Dropping Parentheses for a Single-Parameter Inferred Type

```
friends.forEach(name -> System.out.println(name));
```

The parentheses () around the parameter are optional if the lambda expression takes only one parameter and its type is inferred. We could write name -> ... or (name) -> ...; lean toward the first since it's less noisy.

Creating a Multi-Parameter Lambda Expression

```
friends.stream()
     .reduce((name1, name2) ->
        name1.length() >= name2.length() ? name1 : name2);
```

The parentheses () around the parameter list are required if the lambda expression takes multiple parameters or no parameters.

Calling a Method with Mixed Parameters

```
friends.stream()
     .reduce("Steve", (name1, name2) ->
        name1.length() >= name2.length() ? name1 : name2);
```

Methods can have a mixture of regular classes, primitive types, and functional interfaces as parameters. Any parameter of a method may be a functional interface, and we can send a lambda expression or a method reference as an argument in its place.

Storing a Lambda Expression

```
final Predicate<String> startsWithN = name -> name.startsWith("N");
```

To aid reuse and to avoid duplication, we often want to store lambda expressions in variables.

Creating a Multiline Lambda Expression

```
FileWriterEAM.use("eam2.txt", writerEAM -> {
    writerEAM.writeStuff("how");
    writerEAM.writeStuff("sweet");
});
```

We should keep the lambda expressions short, but it's easy to sneak in a few lines of code. We have to pay penance by using curly braces {}, and the return keyword is required if the lambda expression is expected to return a value.

Returning a Lambda Expression

```
public static Predicate<String> checkIfStartsWith(final String letter) {
    return name -> name.startsWith(letter);
}
```

If a method's return type is a functional interface, we can return a lambda expression from within its implementation.

Returning a Lambda Expression from a Lambda Expression

```
final Function<String, Predicate<String>> startsWithLetter =
    letter -> name -> name.startsWith(letter);
```

We can build lambda expressions that themselves return lambda expressions. The implementation of the Function interface here takes in a String letter and returns a lambda expression that conforms to the Predicate interface.

Lexical Scoping in Closures

```
public static Predicate<String> checkIfStartsWith(final String letter) {
    return name -> name.startsWith(letter);
}
```

From within a lambda expression we can access variables that are in the enclosing method's scope. For example, the variable letter in the checkIfStartsWith()

is accessed within the lambda expression. Lambda expressions that bind to variables in enclosing scopes are called *closures.*

Passing a Method Reference of an Instance Method

```
friends.stream()
       .map(String::toUpperCase);
```

We can replace a lambda expression with a method reference if it directly routes the parameter as a target to a simple method call. The preceding sample code is equivalent to this:

```
friends.stream()
       .map(name -> name.toUpperCase());
```

Passing a Method Reference to a static Method

```
str.chars()
   .filter(Character::isDigit);
```

We can replace a lambda expression with a method reference if it directly routes the parameter as an argument to a static method. The preceding sample code is equivalent to this:

```
str.chars()
   .filter(ch -> Character.isDigit(ch));
```

Passing a Method Reference to a Method on Another Instance

```
str.chars()
   .forEach(System.out::println);
```

We can replace a lambda expression with a method reference if it directly routes the parameter as an argument to a method on another instance; for example, println() on System.out. The preceding sample code is equivalent to this:

```
str.chars()
   .forEach(ch -> System.out.println(ch));
```

Passing a Reference of a Method That Takes Parameters

```
people.stream()
       .sorted(Person::ageDifference)
```

We can replace a lambda expression with a method reference if it directly routes the first parameter as a target of a method call, and the remaining parameters as this method's arguments. The preceding sample code is equivalent to this:

```
people.stream()
      .sorted((person1, person2) -> person1.ageDifference(person2))
```

Using a Constructor Reference

```
Supplier<Heavy> supplier = Heavy::new;
```

Instead of invoking a constructor, we can ask the Java compiler to create the calls to the appropriate constructor from the concise constructor-reference syntax. These work much like method references, except they refer to a constructor and they result in object instantiation. The preceding sample code is equivalent to this:

```
Supplier<Heavy> supplier = () -> new Heavy();
```

Function Composition

```
symbols.map(StockUtil::getPrice)
      .filter(StockUtil.isPriceLessThan(500))
      .reduce(StockUtil::pickHigh)
      .get();
```

We can compose functions to transform objects through a series of operations like in this example. In the functional style of programming, function composition or chaining is a very powerful construct to implement associative operations.

Web Resources

Cutting-stock problem . . . . . . http://en.wikipedia.org/wiki/Cutting_stock_problem
An optimization problem that can use the memoization technique.

Dependency inversion principle . . http://c2.com/cgi/wiki?DependencyInversionPrinciple
Describes a way to realize extensibility by coupling a class to an abstraction (interface) rather than to its implementation.

Don't Repeat Yourself . . . . http://c2.com/cgi/wiki?DontRepeatYourself
I'll let the reader refer to that URL, in the spirit of DRY.

Essence vs. ceremony http://tinyurl.com/b99g2fl
Stuart Halloway discusses essence versus ceremony in this excellent blog entry. The direct URL is http://thinkrelevance.com/blog/2008/04/01/ending-legacy-code-in-our-lifetime.

***Execute around method* pattern** . . . http://c2.com/cgi/wiki?ExecuteAroundMethod
Describes a pattern to control the flow of logic through pre and post operations.

Java 8 JDK https://jdk8.java.net/download.html
Download link for the Java 8 JDK for various operating systems.

Java 8 JDK Documentation http://download.java.net/jdk8/docs/api
JDK documentation with updates for Java 8.

JDK 8 source code . . . . http://hg.openjdk.java.net
JDK 8 source-code download page.

"Lambda: A Peek under the Hood" http://tinyurl.com/abbonw4
A presentation by Brian Goetz at the JavaOne 2012 conference. The direct
URL is https://oracleus.activeevents.com/connect/search.ww?event=javaone#loadSearch-
event=javaone&searchPhrase=Goetz&searchType=session.

Loan pattern . . . . https://wiki.scala-lang.org/display/SYGN/Loan
A discussion of the loan pattern in Scala.

MapReduce . . . . http://research.google.com/archive/mapreduce.html
"MapReduce: Simplified Data Processing on Large Clusters"—a paper by Jeffrey
Dean and Sanjay Ghemawat that discusses this programming model.

Open/closed principle . . . . http://en.wikipedia.org/wiki/Open/closed_principle
Describes Bertrand Meyer's open/closed principle, which states that software
modules must be open for extension, but without having to go through a code
change.

Premature optimization . . . . http://c2.com/cgi/wiki?PrematureOptimization
A web page that discusses the perils of premature optimization.

Tell, Don't Ask . . . . http://pragprog.com/articles/tell-dont-ask
A column that discusses the "Tell, Don't Ask" principle.

"Test Driving Multithreaded Code" http://tinyurl.com/ab5up2w
Code samples from a presentation on unit testing for thread safety. The direct
URL is https://www.agiledeveloper.com/presentations/TestDrivingMultiThreadedCode.zip.

Web page for this book http://www.pragprog.com/titles/vsjava8
This book's web page, with full source-code listings.

Bibliography

[AS96]   Harold Abelson and Gerald Jay Sussman. *Structure and Interpretation of Computer Programs*. MIT Press, Cambridge, MA, 2nd, 1996.

[Blo08]   Joshua Bloch. *Effective Java*. Addison-Wesley, Reading, MA, 2008.

[GHJV95]   Erich Gamma, Richard Helm, Ralph Johnson, and John Vlissides. *Design Patterns: Elements of Reusable Object-Oriented Software*. Addison-Wesley, Reading, MA, 1995.

[Goe06]   Brian Goetz. *Java Concurrency in Practice*. Addison-Wesley, Reading, MA, 2006.

[HT00]   Andrew Hunt and David Thomas. *The Pragmatic Programmer: From Journeyman to Master*. Addison-Wesley, Reading, MA, 2000.

[Sub11]   Venkat Subramaniam. *Programming Concurrency on the JVM: Mastering Synchronization, STM, and Actors*. The Pragmatic Bookshelf, Raleigh, NC and Dallas, TX, 2011.

[Zin01]   William Zinsser. *On Writing Well, 25th Anniversary: The Classic Guide to Writing Nonfiction*. HarperResource, New York, NY, USA, 2001.

Index

More JVM Languages

Check out these other groovy languages for the JVM environment, including Groovy, Scala, and Clojure.

Programming Groovy 2

Groovy brings you the best of both worlds: a flexible, highly productive, agile, dynamic language that runs on the rich framework of the Java Platform. Groovy preserves the Java semantics and extends the JDK to give you true dynamic language capabilities. *Programming Groovy 2* will help you, the experienced Java developer, learn and take advantage of the latest version of this rich dynamic language. You'll go from the basics of Groovy to the latest advances in the language, including options for type checking, tail-call and memoization optimizations, compile time metaprogramming, and fluent interfaces to create DSLs.

Venkat Subramaniam
(370 pages) ISBN: 9781937785307. $35
http://pragprog.com/book/vslg2

Functional Programming Patterns in Scala and Clojure

Solve real-life programming problems with a fraction of the code that pure object-oriented programming requires. Use Scala and Clojure to solve in-depth problems and see how familiar object-oriented patterns can become more concise with functional programming and patterns. Your code will be more declarative, with fewer bugs and lower maintenance costs.

Michael Bevilacqua-Linn
(250 pages) ISBN: 9781937785475. $36
http://pragprog.com/book/mbfpp

Seven in Seven

From web frameworks to concurrency models, see what the rest of the world is doing with this introduction to seven different approaches.

Seven Web Frameworks in Seven Weeks

Whether you need a new tool or just inspiration, *Seven Web Frameworks in Seven Weeks* explores modern options, giving you a taste of each with ideas that will help you create better apps. You'll see frameworks that leverage modern programming languages, employ unique architectures, live client-side instead of server-side, or embrace type systems. You'll see everything from familiar Ruby and JavaScript to the more exotic Erlang, Haskell, and Clojure.

Jack Moffitt, Fred Daoud
(302 pages) ISBN: 9781937785635. $38
http://pragprog.com/book/7web

Seven Concurrency Models in Seven Weeks

Your software needs to leverage multiple cores, handle thousands of users and terabytes of data, and continue working in the face of both hardware and software failure. Concurrency and parallelism are the keys, and *Seven Concurrency Models in Seven Weeks* equips you for this new world. See how emerging technologies such as actors and functional programming address issues with traditional threads and locks development. Learn how to exploit the parallelism in your computer's GPU and leverage clusters of machines with Map-Reduce and Stream Processing. And do it all with the confidence that comes from using tools that help you write crystal clear, high-quality code.

Paul Butcher
(300 pages) ISBN: 9781937785659. $38
http://pragprog.com/book/pb7con

Put the "Fun" in Functional

Elixir puts the "fun" back into functional programming, on top of the robust, battle-tested, industrial-strength environment of Erlang.

Programming Elixir

You want to explore functional programming, but are put off by the academic feel (tell me about monads just one more time). You know you need concurrent applications, but also know these are almost impossible to get right. Meet Elixir, a functional, concurrent language built on the rock-solid Erlang VM. Elixir's pragmatic syntax and built-in support for metaprogramming will make you productive and keep you interested for the long haul. This book is *the* introduction to Elixir for experienced programmers.

Dave Thomas
(240 pages) ISBN: 9781937785581. $36
http://pragprog.com/book/elixir

Programming Erlang (2nd edition)

A multi-user game, web site, cloud application, or networked database can have thousands of users all interacting at the same time. You need a powerful, industrial-strength tool to handle the really hard problems inherent in parallel, concurrent environments. You need Erlang. In this second edition of the best-selling *Programming Erlang*, you'll learn how to write parallel programs that scale effortlessly on multicore systems.

Joe Armstrong
(548 pages) ISBN: 9781937785536. $42
http://pragprog.com/book/jaerlang2

Be Agile

Don't just "do" agile; you want to *be* agile. We'll show you how.

Practices of an Agile Developer

Want to be a better developer? This book collects the personal habits, ideas, and approaches of successful agile software developers and presents them in a series of short, easy-to-digest tips.

You'll learn how to improve your software development process, see what real agile practices feel like, avoid the common temptations that kill projects, and keep agile practices in balance.

Venkat Subramaniam and Andy Hunt
(208 pages) ISBN: 9780974514086. $29.95
http://pragprog.com/book/pad

The Agile Samurai

Here are three simple truths about software development:

1. You can't gather all the requirements up front.
2. The requirements you do gather will change.
3. There is always more to do than time and money will allow.

Those are the facts of life. But you can deal with those facts (and more) by becoming a fierce software-delivery professional, capable of dispatching the most dire of software projects and the toughest delivery schedules with ease and grace.

This title is also available as an audio book.

Jonathan Rasmusson
(280 pages) ISBN: 9781934356586. $34.95
http://pragprog.com/book/jtrap

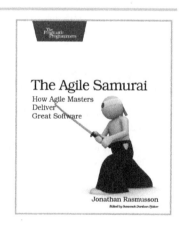

The Pragmatic Bookshelf

The Pragmatic Bookshelf features books written by developers for developers. The titles continue the well-known Pragmatic Programmer style and continue to garner awards and rave reviews. As development gets more and more difficult, the Pragmatic Programmers will be there with more titles and products to help you stay on top of your game.

Visit Us Online

This Book's Home Page
http://pragprog.com/book/vsjava8
Source code from this book, errata, and other resources. Come give us feedback, too!

Register for Updates
http://pragprog.com/updates
Be notified when updates and new books become available.

Join the Community
http://pragprog.com/community
Read our weblogs, join our online discussions, participate in our mailing list, interact with our wiki, and benefit from the experience of other Pragmatic Programmers.

New and Noteworthy
http://pragprog.com/news
Check out the latest pragmatic developments, new titles and other offerings.

Save on the eBook

Save on the eBook versions of this title. Owning the paper version of this book entitles you to purchase the electronic versions at a terrific discount.

PDFs are great for carrying around on your laptop—they are hyperlinked, have color, and are fully searchable. Most titles are also available for the iPhone and iPod touch, Amazon Kindle, and other popular e-book readers.

Buy now at *http://pragprog.com/coupon*

Contact Us

Online Orders:	*http://pragprog.com/catalog*
Customer Service:	*support@pragprog.com*
International Rights:	*translations@pragprog.com*
Academic Use:	*academic@pragprog.com*
Write for Us:	*http://pragprog.com/write-for-us*
Or Call:	+1 800-699-7764

CPSIA information can be obtained at www.ICGtesting.com
Printed in the USA
LVOW03s2041220714

395500LV00027B/197/P